napa bulletin 17

Practicing Anthropology in a Postmodern World: Lessons and Insights from Federal Contract Research

■ Michael C. Reed, ed.

National Association for the Practice of Anthropology
A section of the American Anthropological Association

NAPA Bulletins are occasional publications of the National Association for the Practice of Anthropology, a section of the American Anthropological Association.

Pamela Amoss and Ralph J. Bishop
General Editors

Library of Congress Cataloging-in-Publication Data

Practicing anthropology in a postmodern world: Lessons and insisghts from federal contract research / Michael C. Reed, ed.
p. cm.—(NAPA bulletin; 17)
Includes bibliographical references.
ISBN 0-913167-81-9
1. Applied anthropology—United States. 2. Business anthropology—United States. 3. Research and development contracts, Government— United States. I. Reed, Michael Charles, 1951–. II. Series.
GN560.U6P73 1997
301—dc21 97-6539
CIP

ISBN 0-913167-81-9

Contents

Introduction

Michael C. Reed

The anthropological consulting roles described in this volume need to be seen within the larger context of anthropology's long association with the federal government. This association has included 19th-century ties with the Smithsonian Institution's Bureau of American Ethnology, John Collier's service during the 1930s as Commissioner of the Bureau of Indian Affairs (and his creation of the Applied Anthropology Unit), and the government's intensive employment of numerous anthropologists during World War II in such institutions as the War Relocation Authority, the Civil Affairs Training Schools, and the Office of War Information.

Now, as then, "The great problem for the anthropologist is defining his role. Frequently, busy administrators seek a 'magic' solution to complex problems that may be badly defined or look to the social scientist as a man who must come up with an 'answer' out of a supposed fund of knowledge" (Kennard and MacGregor 1953:839). Herr's commentary (this volume) describes administrators and "hard" scientists who, in a last-gasp effort to find meaningful results, ask anthropologists to come in and "massage" the "qualitative" data. I too have seen numerous instances of this "magic-seeking" while working at a private research and evaluation firm, instances that I will discuss in Chapter 1.

Today, just as has sporadically been the case over the past century, federal use of ethnography is once again in the air, partly because quantitative research models too often suffer overhyped expectations. Numerous questions are thereby raised, including the following:

How exactly does one remain an anthropologist in hectic work settings scarcely resembling that fabled academic anthropology that shaped our original conception of the discipline? How do we help assure (and document) that local community members actually benefit from (and maintain privacy in the face of) federal social service funding? How should we respond to other qualitative researchers (educators, nurses, psychologists, et cetera) who also now claim to "do ethnography"? Does our traditional academic training prepare us adequately for multiple, often unanticipated career paths? How can anthropologists better educate federal agencies about the distinctive nature of anthropological ethnography, which is both a means and a product—the research methodology ("good for 'collecting data' ") and the resulting text, both complexly informed by cultural theory?

Postmodernist Changes

Today's scenario is "postmodern" because what were once considered safe, traditional anthropological role assumptions (i.e., that ethnographers are "culturally expert" and capable of "fairness" and "objectivity," that members of the studied community know little about formal anthropology, and that fieldwork time is abundant) often no longer pertain in contractual, nonacademic anthropology. Now, increasingly, many professional anthropologists working on federal research contracts must continually negotiate with an array of "stakeholders" (e.g., community members, social service staffs, consultant evaluators based in universities or research firms, grantee agencies, and federal officials) simply to define their roles and responsibilities, which may no longer even be specifically "anthropological."

This volume addresses the fact that the field of anthropology has been changing *structurally* for years in ways that have still not been candidly acknowledged by a discipline that, after all, continues to think (if not act) anachronistically in terms of "four fields" and presents (however implicitly) the role of the tenured (or tenure-seeking), full-time, university-based professor of anthropology as normative and most desirable. This academic anthropologist's horizons include the university (or college), the department, students, committee work, tenure, sabbaticals, publications, and sometimes low salaries.

Such a persistent academic *ideal* seriously conflicts with the working realities confronted by large and growing numbers of practicing anthropologists who continue—for various tangled reasons of history, turf, and inertia—to have lower professional status than the archetypal professor. What we are left with are de facto class and status distinctions (see Cassell 1995; Johnston 1995) within anthropology that, I believe, should have no place in a discipline that has long claimed that it was interested in—and has even championed—the underdog.

Baer, in a special issue of *Practicing Anthropology* (volume 17, number 1–2), writes:

> While as a critical anthropologist I may be able to understand elitist practices and attitudes on the part of my "mainstream" anthropological colleagues, I find them inexcusable on the part of my fellow critical anthropologists. Much of the Academic Left has preached egalitarianism while practicing elitism. [1995:43]

In the same issue, Singer states this even more explicitly:

> The end result is the creation of hierarchy and elitism in a field whose self-claimed holism, relativism, and cross-cultural character have been used to critique inequality and domination elsewhere. This situation suggests that the gap between what people believe and what they actually do, between the ideal and the real as we used to call it, applies no less to anthropologists that to those they study. [1995:46]

Today anthropological training in graduate departments continues too often to proceed *as though* new PhDs would still be able to secure traditional academic employment, thereby ignoring the demonstrable fact that this has not been the case for years. Johnston maintains that these departments must bear "ultimate responsibility for the employability of our students"; that is, they must address "educating workers, not just training anthropologists" (1995:48).

The fact of the matter is that anthropology needs to become much more adept at "self-reflexivity," a skill that has long been applauded but less often practiced (see Hymes 1972; Ruby 1982). Otherwise, a sizable blind spot (anthropology's own institutional structures, philosophies, and assumptions) remains for us. Baer (1995) recommends that anthropology reduce its own elitism by conducting anthropological research "on our own associations, conferences, pecking orders, departments, and mythology, as well as on the colleges and universities within which many, but by no means all, of us work" (1995:43).

For applied or practicing anthropologists, such as those doing federal contract research, their own roles, labors, and interpretive styles are inevitably contingent upon a different, less familiar, and often more multivocal and problematic context.[1] The university remains a critical touchstone, even if only in absentia, but a second key reference is the much-maligned U.S. federal government, which looms large. Often perceived as inept or misguided, the federal government nevertheless has the compensating virtues of experience, wealth, and (often) an activist social conscience.

It appears that anthropology today has no guarantee of continued professional existence as universities downsize, some fields preempt our lingo ("ethnographic," "culture," "participant-observation") while others deplore our "soft" methods, tourism encompasses the globe, and "primitives" vanish forever. Not much longer will anthropology be able to just wing it on an exotic smile and a tall tale, since we have lost our monopoly of cultural strangeness.

Differentiating Academic, Applied, and Practicing Anthropology

I have found it useful to try to maintain the tripartite distinction—academic, applied, and practicing anthropology—that has recently been addressed by Baba (1994).[2] According to my understanding of this admittedly idealized typology (since many anthropologists have overlapping roles), academic anthropologists work full-time in a college or university and derive no other substantial income from "outside" work. Applied anthropologists are people who, although university-based (meaning that their academic position is also their primary work role), also work outside the university with some regularity, perhaps, for example, as consultants for county government or the World Bank. Finally, practicing anthropologists do anthropology entirely outside the academic setting. (In fact, applied and practicing anthropologists often engage in, side by side, the very same consulting work.)

It should be noted that this distinction refers not to how, why, and with what theoretical apparatus anthropology is applied to practical problems but rather to the actual employment status of the anthropologist. In other words, as Baba (1994) makes clear, these are *occupational* role definitions that maintain that *where* and *how* you do your anthropology are quite as important factors as, say, what your goals or theoretical stance are.

In contrast, Foster states that applied anthropologists "could describe their professional activities in programs that have as their primary goals changes in human behavior believed to ameliorate contemporary social, economic, and technological problems, rather than the development of social and cultural theory" (1969:54). Appealing though this definition may be, it says nothing about the *workplace* or *professional circumstances* of the anthropologists themselves. The anthropological researcher's occupation per se was not a critical variable for Foster, writing in 1969 in the midst of those academic "golden years," since virtually all anthropologists then worked in academia either full- or part-time.

We, however, believe today that these grounded occupational realities *are* critical variables, just as they have been for most humans throughout history. It no longer suffices to define anthropologists by checking off their "theoretical interests" or "regional specialties." The point is that *where* and *how* one does one's daily labor is a fundamental reality that risks being "fetishized" (to modify a Marxist concept) when we start defining types of anthropologists *only* in terms of, say, "theory preferences." Just as Marx contended that religion exemplifies fetishization because in it "people bestow upon some entity an imaginary power" (Bottomore 1983:165), so anthropology is fetishized if we imagine that a theoretical approach (and not bread-and-butter livelihood) defines the anthropologist. As Agar states, "power and resources [are] steering us all" (p. 86).

This, once again, is true for humans everywhere, including all those legions of "natives" and "indigenes" and "peasants" studied by us for the past century: daily occupation goes a long way toward shaping each individual's distinctive ethos, worldview, and subculture. Would we imagine that it is any different for us? If so, we are engaging in mystification and false consciousness, as Cassell (1995:43) emphasizes in her related discussion of caste and class in the anthropological profession.

Following from this academic/applied/practicing typology, two of this volume's six main authors (Corsica and Payne-Jackson) are applied anthropologists, while the other four are practicing anthropologists (although, to complicate matters, Camino and McKenna, both of whom work primarily as independent consultants, also have adjunct faculty roles at universities). Meanwhile, Herr is a practicing anthropologist while Agar is somewhere in transition between applied and practicing anthropology.

In the following chapters, at least two anthropological roles are introduced that may confound this tripartite typology. McKenna develops the idea of the "contract ethnographer," whose often ambiguous role is similar to but also (according to the author) different from that of the practicing anthropologist. McKenna argues that the contract ethnographer, unlike the practicing anthropologist (or, for that matter, the applied anthropologist), is (most frustratingly) usually only requested to *describe problems* and must leave it to others to solve them and to develop policy.

Meanwhile, Camino discusses the role of the "ethnographic evaluator." These persons, she states, "are expected to go a step beyond description, analysis, and interpretation . . . in order to answer the question: what do these findings mean for policy decision making?" Furthermore, they are required (as we have seen above) to actually evaluate programs and to make formal recommendations about what is to be done.

These two roles seem rather different to me from the "site visitor" role described at the beginning of Chapter 1, one that officially called for some fairly straightforward (and noncontroversial) observing and reporting. It seems to me that McKenna and Camino's roles are best understood as *situational* roles that might, depending upon the circumstances of the particular contract on which one worked, be assumed by either an applied or a practicing anthropologist. It is also true that the "site visitor" role that was filled with consultant ethnographers varied somewhat from site to site, depending upon such things as the openness of the local project director, the preferences of that site's FPO (federal project officer), and indeed, the desires of the site visitor.

I am skeptical of McKenna's contention that the practicing anthropologist is essentially a different beast from the contract ethnographer or that the former has substantially greater freedom to help shape policy than does the latter. I look at the contract ethnographer described by McKenna, and what I see is simply one variation—and a not particularly unexpected one—on the diverse kinds of work done every day by practicing anthropologists.

My own experience with federal contract work is that practicing anthropologists' skills are often underused by funding agencies and that anthropologists are generally used only as "data collectors." But I am also aware that many of my coauthors in this volume have had more years of experience than I have had in working with the federal government. Therefore, when Camino claims that the "ethnographic evaluator" is given great latitude to tell the truth and shape future policy, I know that this has been her experience on other contracts (although it was certainly not the case with the Department of Health and Human Services' Center for Substance Abuse Prevention-High Risk Youth (CSAP-HRY) contract examined in this volume). As for the issue of *who* gets to use the information (collected by consultant ethnographers) to "make policy," it is, once again, my limited experience that more times than not *nobody* uses the information (i.e., most reports by practicing anthropologists are submitted, that fact is recorded, and they are then shelved). But Camino and others have done work on other federal contracts in which their reporting was indeed utilized by policy makers.

Genesis of this Volume

This volume's six chapter authors are anthropologists who became acquainted with each other when they worked together on a federal research contract during 1992–95.[3] The chapters that follow, while often pertaining to this particular contract, also concern other federal contract experiences of the authors.

I am one of these six anthropologists, a full-time employee of a private research firm, CSR Incorporated, that conducted the external evaluation of this federal initiative. The other five anthropologists were employed by CSR as part-time, temporary consultants, to do what was generally termed "ethnographic" or "ethnographic-type" research. Federal contract work of this type is increasingly being done by both applied and practicing anthropologists, and we believe that our experiences might be of interest to a wider audience.

This federal contract involved 64 social service projects in the United States and Puerto Rico,[4] each of which was attempting to prevent the use of alcohol, tobacco, and other drugs (ATOD) by children and adolescents of diverse, often lower-income cultural and socioeconomic groups judged to be living in "high-risk" circumstances. CSR's cross-site evaluation had two major objectives: (1) to determine what interventions were being carried out with what populations and (2) to judge how effective these interventions were in accomplishing their stated ends.

Each project received a CSR site visit involving two persons. A CSR senior staff member (known as the "site evaluator") conducted a five-day visit that focused upon the local project itself (i.e., intervention activities, evaluation instruments, staff interactions) and that resulted in a narrative report.

During that same week, a PhD-level CSR consultant (known as the "site visitor"[5]) began what would usually be a 10-to-12-day visit (sometimes called "brief ethnography") that "examine[d] the community context within which the program operates (sociological, economic, and political) and then focuses on the characteristics, values, cultural norms, and other aspects of the youth and families in the program in relation to the interventions offered" (CSR Incorporated 1993:4). In short, these two persons' visits *overlapped* for the first five days (usually Monday through Friday). Then, on Friday, the site evaluator left to return to Washington, DC, while the site visitor remained on site for another week, usually leaving on the evening of the following Friday. (For a further discussion of these work roles, see "Working on a Federal Research Contract" on page 14.)

It should be pointed out that the site visitor's task was not, strictly speaking, *evaluative* at all, but rather *descriptive*: to review in advance relevant files and written materials, to go on-site to use what were broadly termed "ethnographic methods" (e.g., interviews, participant observation, photography, focus groups), and finally, to write up a detailed narrative report that documented contextual factors.[6] While several of this volume's authors (e.g., Levis-Pilz, Payne-Jackson and Corsica, and Camino) refer explicitly to evaluator roles assumed by anthropologists, these references usually encompass other federal research contracts on which they have been employed.

The rest of this introduction summarizes the chapters, reanalyzes the meaning of academic, applied, and practicing anthropology role distinctions, and finally, considers how federal contract work of this sort fits into our postmodern world.

Chapter Summaries

This volume's five chapters are arranged in two broad clusters: the first three chapters look primarily at applied and practicing anthropological roles, while the next two chapters address specific dilemmas encountered when doing federal contract research.

My chapter attempts to clarify what it was like serving in my particular role with the federal research contract in question: was I able to "herd (anthropological) cats"? Was I able to persuade (however gently, since my managerial role was quite limited) everyone (anthropological and nonanthropological consultants as well as fellow CSR staff members) to work together on a team? I also discuss nine anthropological roles that function today, ranging from the full-time academic professor to the anthropologist employed by a federal agency. I maintain that *anthropology-as-profession* (i.e., something *practically relevant* to the wider public) needs much more serious development in method and theory: heavily ironic postmodernist texts are fun stuff, "but we do not have the luxury of stopping there, nor should society at large be expected to anticipate nothing more from anthropology than . . . clever sarcasm" (p. 25).

Margaret McKenna's chapter addresses the "role uncertainties and ambiguous normative expectations" (p. 29) of anthropologists who serve in what she calls the "contract ethnographer" role.[7] Such research can be quite frustrating to a classically trained ethnographer since the research questions are usually inherited and often poorly framed, the time on site is very brief, and the resulting written report is quickly taken over by others with their own research or political agendas. Nor, according to the author, is the contract ethnographer—a role, McKenna maintains, that is essentially different from that of the practicing anthropologist—allowed to make recommendations that shape policy. The author concludes that the motto,

"Offend no one," which often applies to this type of work, may be antithetical to many anthropological instincts.

Linda Camino attempts to decipher the presently ambiguous nature of "ethnography" (applied to program evaluation), a field methodology seized by many. In this welter of often conflicting claims, is there anything distinctively valuable about *anthropological* ethnography and "these deceptively simple methods" that we use? The author reviews five areas of "preadaptive" anthropological knowledge and experience and concludes that a viable anthropology-as-profession requires us to make more explicit to the public the practical merits of what we do. Referring to the "ethnographic evaluator" role, she maintains (in contrast to McKenna) that this role *requires* the anthropologist to make recommendations. She also advises that policy makers have little interest merely in rich, "thick" description. Rather, a "description-analysis-interpretation trinity" is called for, as is anthropologists' willingness to *evaluate* and to make *recommendations.*

Gladys Levis-Pilz takes us with pained humor through an actual site visit and the not-uncommon experience of the initially self-confident researcher getting all tangled up in unforeseen stakeholder issues and tensions. She was vividly reminded that *being analyzed on the printed page* (something that ethnographers usually initiate rather than receive) often hurts. In effect, "a very complex situation was made to appear simple. A greater effort should have been made to negotiate the parameters of the undertaking, to reconcile the multiple stakeholder perspectives, and to assess the true willingness of project personnel to host the site visit" (p. 67).

Today's rage, "political correctness" (or PC), is scrutinized by Arvilla Payne-Jackson and Joanne Corsica, both of whom are concerned about the federal tendency to "ration" research slots according to some preconceived, superficial notion of appropriate ethnic and racial "matching" between the researcher and the local site. We all know how much more intense *intra-* group differences can be than those between groups: what appears clear from afar (i.e., "a working class Hispanic neighborhood") becomes very complicated when seen up close with its multiple crosscutting, confounding racial, ethnic, and cultural identities (so much for the utility of the generic term *Hispanic*). The authors write, "Such PC practices completely overlook the fact that anthropologists are trained to be able to live and communicate effectively with people from different cultures" (p. 70).

Phillip R. Herr and Michael Agar comment on the preceding chapters and issues. Herr's several years' work for the General Accounting Office (GAO) provide him with a unique vantage point. His anecdotes are particularly absorbing: stories of the two quantitative evaluators who, in some desperation, sought at the last minute to obtain anthropological "insights" since "the numbers" were not offering many. Herr also muses on the possible difficulties of trying to *manage* anthropologists (as in team research).

Agar, who has unconventionally and successfully mixed academic and applied careers for over two decades, resonates to the role of the paradoxical postmodernist, betwixt and between, by turns ironic, earnest, and muckraking. As he himself sets out on a new career, leaving academia "as a one-man think tank," he observes: "What we are left with is a view of a field that 'decanonizes' the ivory tower, renders it more permeable, and elevates the knowledge and experience of those working at a distance from it" (p. 90). That summarizes well what this volume is about.

Notes

Acknowledgments. This volume originated as a NAPA-invited session, entitled "Applied Ethnography in a 'Postmodern' World: Negotiating Stakeholder and Anthropologist Rights in Federal Contract Research," presented on December 3, 1994, at the AAA meeting in Atlanta, GA. This session was co-organized by Michael Reed, Dorothy Angell, Linda Camino, and Arvilla Payne-Jackson. Mike Agar and Phil Herr generously offered to serve both as session and, later, volume discussants. We would like to thank both NAPA and Peter Van Arsdale for helping to arrange that AAA session. Our appreciation to Shirley Fiske for attending the session and recommending it to NAPA as a NAPA Bulletin. Thanks to Pamela Amoss for serving as a capable general editor and to the several anonymous reviewers both of our original proposal and of the completed manuscript. Although I took the lead as editor, this volume is a collaborative effort, and I want to thank each of the chapter authors for their contributions. My special thanks to Linda Camino for her conversations (usually over the phone) with me during the past couple years. Thanks to Judith De Jong, former federal project officer of the CSAP-HRY Demonstration Grant, who supported ethnographic research (and whose great-uncle went to do mission work among the Zuni a century ago). Thanks to CSR's David Fairweather and Bill Scarbrough who, each in turn, ran the CSAP-HRY contract and took ethnographic work seriously. My appreciation to Jim MacDonald for guiding us through the *askSam* thicket. Finally, I would like to thank Sherrie Aitken, president of CSR Incorporated, for (a) hiring me, (b) always paying me promptly and fully, and not incidentally, (c) encouraging the regular use of both anthropologists and ethnographic research methods for the evaluation of federally funded social service programs.

1. This is not to underestimate the complexity of the anthropology professor's periodic fieldwork research, since fieldwork is always "multivocal and problematic." But this academically based professor is, on average, rarely in the field but generally in the university department or classroom, arenas that are, however challenging, by now thoroughly familiar "home turf." In contrast, the practicing anthropologist is always "in the field."

2. Baba (1994) notes that, prior to the mid-1970s, virtually *all* anthropologists were based in academe, even those conducting extended periods of applied work. The founding of NAPA in 1983 "represented the declaration of non-academic anthropology as a distinct and legitimate *occupation* in its own right, separate in professional identity from the role of traditional applied academic anthropology" (Baba 1994:175). Applied anthropology itself dates back to the founding of the Society for Applied Anthropology (SfAA) at Harvard University in April 1941. The founders, Eliot Chapple and John Provinse, believed that anthropologists should be used to solve administrative problems within public and private institutions (Partridge and Eddy 1987:39; Spicer 1976). In Britain, until very recently, academic anthropologists and applied anthropologists were the only two relevant categories, with the "no longer anthropologist" category filled by what we in the United States would term "practicing anthropologists" (Grimshaw and Hart 1995:67).

3. Much of the research described in this introduction and in Chapters 1–5 was done under the auspices of CSR Incorporated's contract with the United States Department of Health and Human Services' Center for Substance Abuse Prevention-High Risk Youth (CSAP-HRY) Demonstration Grant. This contract was completed on September 30, 1995.

4. Throughout this volume we try to distinguish *programs* (i.e., large and sometimes national initiatives) from *projects* (i.e., local site-based organizations where programs are actually implemented), with the latter term being used most frequently. The "umbrella agencies" that often sponsor individual projects are often called grantees or grantee agencies, since these entities officially receive the federal grant money. But to complicate matters,

local projects also, of course, implement their own *interventions* or *programs,* and this latter term is often confused with the previous, overarching sense of "program."

5. This role was originally called "ethnographer," but this was dropped because it implied that only persons formally trained in ethnography (i.e., anthropologists) were qualified to serve in the role. CSR sought to hire "qualitative researchers" from multiple fields.

6. CSR maintained that the site visitor's report "provides the conceptual and empirical bridge that links the process evaluation and the intervention effects" (CSR Incorporated 1993:31).

7. It should be remembered that the official role title held by these consultants was simply "site visitor." Therefore, when McKenna speaks of "contract ethnographer" or Camino or Payne-Jackson and Corsica refer to the "ethnographic evaluator," they are coining new terms.

References Cited

Baba, Marietta L.
1994 The Fifth Discipline: Anthropological Practice and the Future of Anthropology. Human Organization 53(2):174–185.

Baer, Hans A.
1995 Commentary: Elitism and Discrimination within Anthropology. Practicing Anthropology 17(1–2):42–43.

Bottomore, Tom, ed.
1983 A Dictionary of Marxist Thought. Cambridge, MA: Harvard University Press.

Cassell, Joan
1995 Cast and Class in Anthropology. Practicing Anthropology 17(1–2):43–44.

CSR Incorporated
1993 Procedures Manual for On Site Visits to CSAP High Risk Youth Demonstration Grants. Revised edition. Washington, DC: CSR Incorporated.

Foster, George M.
1969 Applied Anthropology. Boston: Little, Brown.

Grimshaw, Anna, and Keith Hart
1995 The Rise and Fall of Scientific Ethnography. *In* The Future of Anthropology: Its Relevance to the Contemporary World. Akbar S. Ahmed and Cris N. Shore, eds. Pp. 46–64. London: Athlone.

Hymes, Dell, ed.
1972 Reinventing Anthropology. New York: Random House.

Johnston, Barbara R.
1995 Notes and Reflections on Life in the Margins. Practicing Anthropology 17(1/2):46–48.

Kennard, Edward A., and Gordon MacGregor
1953 Applied Anthropology in Government: United States. *In* Anthropology Today: An Encyclopedic Inventory. Pp. 832–840. Chicago: University of Chicago Press.

Partridge, William L., and Elizabeth M. Eddy.
1987 The Development of Applied Anthropology in America. *In* Applied Anthropology in America. 2nd edition. Elizabeth M. Eddy and William L. Partridge, eds. Pp. 3–55. New York: Columbia University Press.

Ruby, Jay, ed.
1982 A Crack in the Mirror: Reflexive Perspectives in Anthropology. Philadelphia: University of Pennsylvania Press.

Singer, Merrill
1995 Reflections on Elitism in American Anthropology. Practicing Anthropology 17(1–2):44–46.

Spicer, Edward H.
1976 Beyond Analysis and Explanation?: Notes on the Life and Times of the Society for Applied Anthropology. Human Organization 35(4):335–343.

Nine Contemporary Anthropological Work Roles

Michael C. Reed

One of this volume's commentators, Phillip R. Herr, has expressed an interest in knowing more about "the coordination and management of anthropologists," an activity that, he suggests, may be like "herding cats." In my experience, the tougher management challenge may be trying to conduct teamwork with professionals from multiple disciplines that usually share very little professional identity. But more on that later.

This chapter will explore this (and other) management issues while looking more broadly at my work role at a for-profit, "inside the Beltway" research and evaluation firm (CSR Incorporated) located in Washington, DC. This is the firm, as noted in the introduction, that had been awarded the federal contract to conduct the external, cross-site evaluation of the 64 drug and alcohol prevention projects. Two-member site visit teams consisting of a CSR site evaluator and a consultant site visitor visited each of these sites.

Having described what it is like for an anthropologist to work at such a research firm, I will then more closely examine my specific role in (1) helping to oversee the site visit teams on this federal contract and (2) heading up the analysis of "qualitative" data (i.e., 20–60 page, double-spaced, narrative reports written by the site evaluators and the site visitors).

Next, I will lay out what I take to be an interrelated system of nine contemporary anthropological work roles (see Figure 1), including my role at CSR, that, I believe, fairly comprehensively describe (at least in outline) the contemporary range of academic, applied, and practicing anthropological roles *as they pertain to federal contract research.* Although many applied and practicing anthropologists work elsewhere (for state or local governments, nonprofits, foundations, or private corporations), the federal government has always been anthropologists' primary nonacademic employer.

Finally, I will propose some ideas about the future of anthropology, a profession that in my view is becoming less relevant today because of its several outdated assumptions and its inability to be more *self-reflective.*

The Anthropologist in a Private Research Firm

My employer (since 1992) is a research and evaluation firm that has been in existence for over 20 years, has about 125 full-time employees, and does virtually all of its work on federal contracts. I am one of two anthropologists among about 25 senior staff members who hold PhDs or EdDs. (The

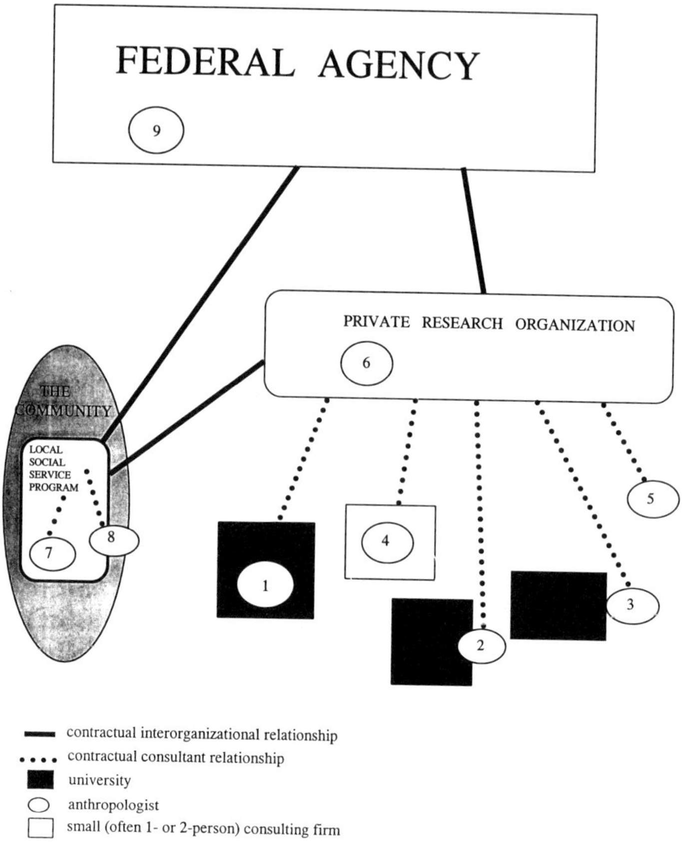

Figure 1. Interrelated system of nine contemporary anthropological work roles. 1 represents a full-time academic; 2, a part-time academic; 3, a marginalist; 4, an entrepreneur; 5, a soloist; 6, a private hire; 7, a resident ethnographer; 8, a visiting ethnographer; and 9, a federal employee.

firm often markets itself as a "small university, but without the university's high overhead.")

A private research firm like this necessarily depends entirely on "soft" grant and contract monies and therefore expends considerable energy each year (the proposal writing "season" may easily run from March until October) on proposal writing in response to RFPs (requests for proposals).[1] Fat years, when numerous new contracts are won, bring new hiring and renewed job security for all. Lean years mean layoffs and downsizing, usually in the early autumn. (The federal fiscal year, like "FY96," typically ends on September 30.) Job security here is a relative thing.

The bottom line here is, quite rightly, "generating new business," and this is accomplished by means of repeated, monthlong bouts of team proposal writing. This work is, of course, *in addition* to whatever ongoing contract work you may already have to do. The proposal writing is usually in response to an announcement identified in the *Commerce Business Daily* or the *Federal Register.* Once the decision has been made to "go for it," and assuming that the sought contract is large enough (i.e., two to five years in duration and worth 750 thousand to several million dollars), the proposal manager convenes a large, 10- to 20-person "kickoff" meeting to review the RFP,[2] draft a tentative writing schedule, make writing assignments, and establish deadlines.

Once the RFP has been carefully studied, the firm (along with any other bidders) usually drafts a formal list of questions about the RFP which is sent to the federal agency. Ideally, the agency promptly provides useful answers to these questions so that the proposal can be more realistically completed. The firm may choose to bid on its own, as a "prime," or as a "sub" to another "prime." The actual monthlong process of researching and writing the proposal often requires that the firm's individual proposal writers become "experts" on a new topic very quickly (three or four days to a week), review and cite the important literature, and take stock of what (if any) previous related work has been done by the firm. If the firm is weak in a particular area, consultants (or even potential new, full-time hires) may be contacted to bolster the effort.

The proposal itself is often a rather massive, perhaps 200- to 400-page bound document with an attractive cover, a technical proposal containing numerous professionally-done graphics, tables, and matrixes, and several appendixes containing supporting material. The budget proposal is submitted under separate cover. Once the proposal is submitted, it may take several weeks or even months before the federal agency notifies the firm either that the firm's proposal is no longer being considered or that the proposal is among the finalists. (Finalists then proceed through a "best-and-final offer" [BAFO] competition.)

Working for such a research firm is satisfying but also tiring, stressful, and year-round. Nine- and ten-hour workdays and weekend work are not uncommon. Deadlines constantly have to be met, and your own contribution is usually just a portion of the total effort, one that will surely be edited and shaped by others. Writing assignments are heavy and multiple, you often do not see your name on the title page, and work efforts are not always promptly rewarded (e.g., you may contribute heavily to writing a given proposal and yet not even be bid as one of the senior project members).

Research efforts are diffuse, politicized, and long in duration. Fieldwork opportunities are usually brief (perhaps two to five days on site) and only occasional (maybe three to four site visits a year). Such work has definite rewards: it is fast-paced, intellectually challenging, and socially relevant. Nevertheless, all in all, it is very different from what they told most of us about in graduate school.

Writing for publication (to further your own professional career) is not a highly rewarded priority for most private firms and, consequently, is basically done out of your own hide in the evening, on an odd Saturday afternoon, or during a rare weeklong vacation. There is little encouragement for submitting your own autonomous article to disciplinary journals. When firms do seek publication, it is usually, once again, a team writing process aimed at problem-focused, interdisciplinary publications (such as the *Quarterly Journal of the Study of Alcohol*). Such writing is often a spin-off (perhaps pushed by the FPO, or Federal Project Officer) from specific federal contracts in an effort to utilize data or new methodologies.

This concept of "teamwork" is essential in such a working environment, and my role as an anthropologist per se is often quite secondary to my usefulness to the firm as a writer, editor, researcher, analyst, or trainer. I suspect (based upon my own occasional difficulties) that it is this requirement to be truly collaborative and to subsume your own ego in a joint effort that causes many anthropologists the most discomfort. Graduate school taught us to revere the autonomous, scholarly article; practical work forces us to value the team effort to achieve a measurable success. We learn to step back, mix it up, and refrain from focusing only on "noble" self-advertisement—not a bad lesson if we intend to further the profession by persuading a wider public that we have something useful to offer.

Working on a Federal Research Contract

This section builds upon information already presented earlier in this chapter and in the introduction. About nine of the approximately 20 consultants in CSR's "pool" of site visitors were anthropologists, while the others were trained in various social science fields.[3] Of these nine anthropologists (all women), two held tenured academic positions and four others, although they held part-time or temporary "adjunct" academic positions, derived most of their income from consulting work. The remaining three anthropologists were full-time consultants, and one of these ran her own small research business. These consultants participated at the start of the contract in a three-day training and meeting to get acquainted with their assigned grantees.

As a full-time CSR employee, I was one of the site evaluators (described in the Introduction) for this federal contract. (The site evaluators were all full-time CSR staff members with MAs or PhDs in varied academic backgrounds, such as education, child psychology, social work, sociology, research, and measurement.)

My tasks were varied. I helped CSR to define the site visitor work role and to prepare their various site visit protocols (such as interview guides and a reporting outline). I also took the lead in developing CSR's procedures for conducting computer-aided analysis (using *askSam* software) of the elaboratively coded qualitative data generated by the contract—that is, narrative reports, one of which was written by each member of the two-person site visit team (see Reed 1995 for a discussion of this analytic process).

I also played the somewhat anomalous role as de facto liaison between CSR and the consultant site visitors, a role that obliged me to look out for CSR's needs (i.e., conducting research and writing reports that met the need of the federal agency) while simultaneously trying to respond to the consultants' requests. This role entailed receiving and processing their reports and expense statements, answering their questions, and serving to the best of my ability as their "advocate" vis-à-vis the research firm and the federal agency. Just as Levis-Pilz refers to feeling "sandwiched between" other players (e.g., the FPO, the local project director, the grantee agency, and CSR) in her role as site visitor, I often found that my liaison role on this federal contract necessitated, as Levis-Pilz writes, that "my work was highly proscribed" (p. 62) and often not particularly anthropological.

It is probably fair to say that almost all of the site visitors, anthropologists and nonanthropologists alike, found such federal contract work to be both appealing (it provided additional income and travel, résumés could be bolstered, and most of the site visitors savored the work's social issues and theoretical implications) and sometimes frustrating. Site visitors' frustrations included the following:

- Noncompetitive consultant rates: Individual federal agencies, subagencies, or even individual agency procurements typically establish their own ceilings for daily consultant rates. For human service agencies, these rates are typically in the $250–450 range, which is low by today's "free market" consulting standards of perhaps $500–1,500 per day (for comparable ethnographic research), often *not* including expenses.[4] For this contract, CSR's site visitors were paid $250 a day.

  Furthermore, it was CSR's own contract regulations, not the federal agency's, which dictated that each site visitor could bill no more than 15 days per site visit, including time on site (usually 10–12 days, including an intervening weekend), time preparing for the site visit, and time to write the report. What eventually happened was that the more conscientious (although perhaps less economically rational) consultants billed the maximum limit and then just took whatever additional time was necessary to write what were often very complex, lengthy reports. These realities soured some consultants, while others accepted them as part of the game.
- Writing to a detailed outline: CSR developed highly structured writing outlines to be used both by the site evaluators and the site visitors. These outlines were keyed to various research and evaluation questions that CSR was responsible for answering. The end result was that these a priori outlines compelled the site visitors (some more willingly than others) to gather information on site to answer specific questions. As time went on, it became apparent that some outline sections and questions were more relevant than others. But bureaucratic processes

being what they are, it was not always easy to amend the writing outline even to improve it. Some consultants probably found the outline a help; many found them to be restrictive and counterintuitive. In any case, this was not "virgin" ethnography, in which unencumbered anthropologists could pursue any and every trail of inspiration.

- Ethnic/gender matching: Payne-Jackson and Corsica's chapter discusses in considerable detail the often onerous process by which FPOs would permit local project managers to influence the selection of their own site visitors.
- Finished report becomes federal property: Having done the preparation, visited the site, and written the report, site visitors were then obliged to relinquish their creation. Some people accepted this as simply part of their contract. Others felt considerable ambivalence about being unable to have any control over how (or even if) their reports were used for future analysis or policy making. Site visitors were entitled to receive a copy of their final reports (which had by this time been thoroughly edited by CSR and reviewed by the project's FPO and the project itself), but only if they explicitly made this request.

This federal contract also generated some frustrations of my own, including:

- Reports that are too long: Although site visitors were instructed to provide CSR with narrative reports that were 20 to 40 double-spaced pages long, some consultants (most of whom—perhaps three out of five—were anthropologists) submitted reports that were closer to 50 or 60 pages in length. It became clear that more is not necessarily better (even when the report was in fact excellent) since CSR's analytic process, which actually required carefully reading and coding all of these reports, often threatened to bog down in the profusion of pages (Reed 1995). The sheer volume of the narratives became a problem, and it often delayed CSR from identifying key issues and findings.
- A highly laborious, nuanced analytic process: I took the lead in helping CSR to develop, over nearly two years, a computer-assisted qualitative text analysis system capable of handling relatively large quantities (for example, 500 or more single-spaced pages) of narrative site evaluator and site visitor reports. We used *askSam* (version 5.1) software to do the reaggregation of precoded text. The firm's entire learning process was long and sometimes tedious as we first analyzed the reports "by hand," identified the need for an appropriate software, had the software customized (by a local anthropologist who also did computer programming), learned how to do textual coding, trained our staff, conceptualized the entire analytic endeavor, and finally, "made sense" of disparate, lengthy new text files built around shared code categories. There is nothing "short and sweet" about this process, and one sweats long and hard for every bit of insight gained.

- "A 'magic' solution to complex problems" (Kennard and MacGregor 1953:839): This passage, drawn from a longer quote found in this volume's introduction, confirms Herr's anecdotal evidence that administrators often look to heretofore ignored anthropologists for last-minute revelation, especially when the "hard data" do not pan out (as seems to be the case time and time again in federal contract research). There is an assumption abroad that "soft," "qualitative" data are both easy to obtain and easy to make sense of. Nothing is further from the truth. Qualitative data are most useful when they can *complement* or *refine our understanding of* statistically obtained information. On the other hand, statistical data are most useful when the questions asked are based on good qualitative analysis.

Nine Contemporary Anthropological Roles

Working on this and several other federal contracts over the past 4½ years has clarified for me a structured universe of diverse anthropological roles that embody that previously mentioned, rather generic typology of "academic," "applied," and "practicing" anthropologists. My aim in this section is to examine some of the complexities of how and why anthropologists work (and reflect) as they do in various work settings. My assumption is, once again, that *occupation* is a fundamental variable that powerfully shapes our anthropological views and theories and, indeed, our understanding of what anthropology is.

In this volume alone, my coauthors and I represent a substantial range of occupational diversity: an assistant (Corsica) and an associate (Payne-Jackson) professor of anthropology, both of whom do considerable consulting; two part-time, adjunct professors of anthropology (Camino) and nursing and health services (McKenna) who, while teaching occasionally, really make their livings from consulting work; the principal of a small consulting firm (Levis-Pilz) who recently left her associate professor position at a university; a full professor of anthropology (Agar) who is in the midst of setting up his own one-man research firm (while still keeping a hand in the university); a full-time employee of the General Accounting Office (Herr); and a full-time employee of a private research and evaluation firm (Reed).

Following are descriptions of a series of nine anthropological roles (see Figure 1), the first of which is based entirely within the university but the rest of which play themselves out ever farther from that place. I have devised the following role titles, which I invite readers to improve: (1) full-time academic; (2) part-time academic; (3) marginalist; (4) entrepreneur; (5) soloist; (6) private hire; (7) resident ethnographer; (8) visiting ethnographer; and (9) federal employee.

Roles 1, 2, and 3, in that order, serve as this analysis's conceptual baseline since they illustrate the process (akin to an egg emerging from the hen) by which anthropologists separate from the university, perhaps tentatively at first, and enter into strange new professional experiences. None of these roles are of entirely recent origin, although roles 4 through 8 were doubtlessly much less common in the past, when the "independent consultant" was rare.

Role 1: Full-Time Academic

This role is the full-time professor entirely devoted to academic work. It was recently observed that the "modal academic anthropologist is a white, male, full professor, nearing retirement, whose principal subfield is sociocultural anthropology" (Givens and Mahaney 1994:4). During the 1993–94 academic year at four-year United States public and private institutions, anthropology faculty earned the following average salaries:[5] full professor, $58,000; associate professor, $44,500; assistant professor, $35,500; new assistant professor, $33,000. Ninety percent of all full-time United States anthropology faculty in 1992–93 were white, with three percent Hispanic, three percent black, two percent Asian, and two percent Native American (Givens and Mahaney 1994).

Women continue to be a minority of anthropology faculty, although their numbers have improved substantially at the entry level: between 1983 and 1987, the number of female assistant professors increased from 38.6 to 48.1 percent. The increases for the associate professor and full professor levels were less encouraging: 27.4 to 29.6 percent and 16.9 to 18.3 percent, respectively (Webster and Burton 1992). My experience with federal contract research suggests that female anthropologists work (often by necessity) as consultants far more often than do men. (See Table 1 for a summary of the professional roles of the members of one local professional organization, or LPO.)

Role 1 may also be conceived of as including those *applied* professors who, although securely "within" academe (i.e., tenured with full benefits), also (as is increasingly common) "moonlight" from time to time; for example, they serve as "expert witnesses" at trials, do summer consulting, or travel abroad occasionally to conduct World Bank evaluative site visits. These professors may prove to be very valuable to the field because they have gained practical (not just theoretical) knowledge of nonacademic anthropology and may thus help to train more savvy new PhDs capable of moving in alternative career directions.

Margaret Mead (1973) noted that one reason why applied anthropology had languished during the 1950s and 1960s was due to

> easily found, well-paying jobs in academia and the realization that anthropology is becoming an academic-based discipline with rather rigid hierarchical relationships, from the prestigious universities, through a series of lower echelons, all academic, and the awareness that the ambitious young anthropologist is likely to be penalized for working outside these frozen hierarchies. [1973:15]

One could not ask for a more succinct explanation of some of the status differences between academic, applied, and practicing anthropologists. If the reader finds my account of academic life incomplete, I invite her or him to look at Agar's piece concluding this volume.

Role 2: Part-Time Academic and Role 3: Marginalist

These two roles reflect differences in degree more than in kind. Depending upon your viewpoint, they represent either a departure *from* (voluntary or not) [2 → 3] or an *entry into* [2 ← 3] the university, although this chapter focuses on the former. These two roles are filled by those liminal individuals who are betwixt and between the academy and the "outside" world. Cassell writes that "academic anthropology is based on a class/caste system" (1992:32) that slots anthropologists into the following, rather quirky, descending status order: (1) those who only have to teach two courses per semester; (2) those who teach three to four courses a semester "at nonelite institutions"; (3) "one-year temporaries"; (4) part-timers; and (5) the unemployed, underemployed, or "hobbyists." I experienced (4) and (5) earlier in my career. Later in this chapter we will examine more closely the situations of under- or unemployed anthropologists.

All of the remaining anthropological roles examined in this chapter (roles 4 through 9) function in that relatively new, nonacademic world that I, for one, never even seriously considered working in while I was in graduate school. I vaguely recall one graduate seminar presentation on "applied anthropology," and I remember being rather nonplussed by *that* unglamorous topic. (By contrast, some squeezed graduate students today, like those belonging to Yale's Graduate Employees Students' Organization [GESO], are trying to change a rather inflexible system.)[6]

Role 4: Entrepreneur

This role represents those increasingly numerous anthropologists who have set up their own often small, home-based consulting firms that pro-

Table 1. Professional Roles of Members of Washington Association of Professional Anthropologists, 1993–95 (WAPA 1993, 1994, 1995)

	1993	1994	1995
All members	286	292	302
With professional affiliations	220	248	263
Federal employees	58 (26.4%)	55 (22.2%)	51 (19.4%)
USAID	16	14	13
National Park Service	8	7	7
Private research/business firms	69 (31.4%)	65 (26.2%)	82 (31.2%)
University faculty/students	56 (25.5%)	82 (33.1%)	91 (34.5)
Independent consultants	9 (all women)	17 (14 women)	18 (13 women)

vide them with professional structure, identification, status, and often shared resources. As Cassell states, "Early on, I learned that it was important to have an institutional affiliation for my name tag at meetings; otherwise, people's eyes tended to glaze over as they looked past my name tag (and me) to find someone interesting and important to talk to" (1992:32). Who among us has never skulked about some decibel-crashing, overcrowded AAA meeting feeling vaguely uneasy about the uncertain implications of those infernal little name tags?[7]

These anthropological entrepreneurs often serve as consultants to federal, state, or local agencies, research firms, or—as is shown in roles 7 and 8—local social service projects. The work of all of these anthropological role-players (i.e., roles 2–9) is strongly influenced by the following reality:

> As neoconservatives observe, funds for the downtrodden "trickle up" and provide public-sector professionals with grants, consultantships, and jobs. More government activism means more lawyers, social workers, teachers, and researchers on the public payroll. More public planning also means more power for academic and government experts. One can debate whether government planning is helpful for society as a whole, but it is certainly a boon . . . for the expert's ego and pocketbook. [Derber and Schwartz 1990:177–178]

It is undoubtedly the case that many practicing anthropologists rely upon a "big government" model in which public monies are spent generously on the sorts of social service agendas that began during Franklin Roosevelt's New Deal, that were intensified during Lyndon Johnson's "Great Society" era, and that are now seriously jeopardized by Republican efforts to scale back government's role and to "block-grant" diminished funds to be used by the states.

Role 5: Soloist

This role may stand for at least two different realities: an unemployed or underemployed anthropologist or an "independent consultant" who does role 4–type labors but without the organizational structure of a formal consulting firm. This unemployed anthropologist may be thought of, hopefully, as "in transition" to any one of the other eight roles. She or he may have willingly (or not) given up on finding academic work and may now be playing the field, sending out applications, networking, finishing a book, writing a grant proposal, or being supported by a spouse.

On the other hand, there are today many anthropology PhDs who, although employed, no longer function professionally as anthropologists, and their work colleagues may not even *know* that they are anthropologists. Many of these people are, unquestionably, pained and frustrated by this situation; after all, most of us would not bother to scrap and struggle to earn a doctorate without the reasonable hope that such an education would provide us with an unambiguous career identity. There are also anthropologists who, I suspect, simply accept this professional anonymity as a condition of "getting out of school, finding work, settling down, and getting older."

Role 6: Private Hire

This role has already been described at the beginning of this chapter.

Role 7: Resident Ethnographer and Role 8: Visiting Ethnographer

These two roles are commonly encountered in federal contract research involving local human service projects. Role 7, for example, might be filled by an anthropologist serving as a project's "resident ethnographer," someone who lives locally, knows the community, perhaps speaks Spanish or Vietnamese, and visits the project twice a week to document project processes and contexts, observe intervention activities, attend staff meetings, conduct client focus groups, and write quarterly reports that are submitted either to the project director or to the federal funding agency or its evaluation contractor.

Role 8, a variation of role 7, might be filled by an anthropologist (often not a local resident) who would occasionally visit the project (perhaps for two three-day site visits annually) to conduct external process evaluations resulting in written reports. Both of these roles are often filled by anthropologists who also perform roles 4 and 5. It is also not uncommon for a college or university professor (role 1) to do this sort of part-time consulting.

Role 9: Federal Employee

Our role analysis finally considers role 9, that of an anthropologist working full-time for the U.S. government.[8] Table 1 provides some results of a study that I have done of the 1993–95 membership of WAPA (discussed earlier).

Several aspects of this table deserve comment:

- Although WAPA's overall membership increased only slightly during this period (286 to 302, or +5.6 percent), the number of members *who voluntarily identified professional affiliations* increased by 19.5 percent (220 to 263). *Comment: WAPA members are, one might speculate, becoming more pragmatic about stating who they are and what they do.*
- The percentage of members employed by the federal government declined by 12.1 percent (58 to 51). *Comment: Unsurprisingly, given the recent Republican takeover of Congress, anthropologist-friendly federal agencies (e.g., Department of Health and Human Services, US-AID) have been laying off, not hiring.*
- Perhaps the most striking change during the three-year period was the 62.5 percent increase (from 56 to 91) in the number of members

(many of them students) declaring university affiliations. *Comment: Graduate students, new PhDs, and faculty may be finding it increasingly worthwhile to become members of an LPO and thereby "network" with professional and employment circles beyond the realm of the university.*

- It is also notable that the number of independent consultants nearly doubled (from nine to 18) and that the majority of these members (all in 1993, 14 in 1994, and 13 in 1995) were women. *Comment: Such consultants—who might occupy any of roles 3 through 5, 7, or 8 in Figure 1—are becoming more common, and they are often women, whose numbers have greatly expanded within the profession but who continue to find it difficult to move up through academia.*

Federally employed anthropologists, like anthropologists in roles 3 through 8, undoubtedly experience the full range of satisfactions and dissatisfactions deriving from a professional anthropological identity: a few function on the job explicitly *as anthropologists,* while others (probably the majority) find that that identity is masked, obscured, or just plain irrelevant. I am not aware that the bureaucratic peculiarities of federal employment are any more conducive to traditional, academy-based anthropological role values—that is, independence, autonomy, time for reflection and writing—than is work in a private research firm or with a local project. Anthropological careers located outside the university are invariably different—sometimes more satisfying, sometimes less so—than those on the inside.

Future of the Anthropology Profession

It is ultimately very important that all anthropologists—academic, applied, and practicing—ponder carefully what it means to be part of the larger collective of anthropologists. For example, is this collective now to be thought of as a *vocation* (a religious-like "calling" shared with relatively few others), a *discipline* (university-based and academic),[9] or a *profession* (outward-looking, PR-conscious, and with an eye on the job market)? Halliday says of his own field of sociology, "It has no discernible clientele outside the academy. It has no monopoly over an area of work." He also notes "an enduring tension between its intellectual integrity as a scholarly discipline and its civic obligations as a public profession" (1992:12,14). Anthropology is surely not immune from such concerns.[10]

Nearly a quarter-century ago, Margaret Mead (1973) lamented anthropology's "excessive growth" and its loss of sense of vocation during the period 1953–73:

> From a tiny scholarly group that could easily be fitted into a couple of buses, and most of whom knew each other, we have grown into a group of tremendous, anonymous milling crowds, meeting at large hotels where there are so many sessions that people do well to find those of their colleagues who are

> interested in the same specialty. Today we look something like the other social science disciplines, suffering some of the same malaise, and becoming cynical about slave markets and worried when grants and jobs seem to be declining. [1973:1]

Similarly, Geertz's take on the field's evolution is as follows: "Once a guild occupation, comparing itself alternately to a tribe, a craft, or a social club, anthropology has become a sprawling consortium of dissimilar scholars held together largely by will and convenience" (Geertz 1995:133). Both Mead and Geertz wax nostalgic over the vanished (invented?) past but are elusive about the present or future.

In 1987 Erve Chambers wrote,

> To my mind, the greatest present irony of applied anthropology is found in the contrast between a *profession,* which looks outward for survival and is careful of its image, and a *discipline,* which must contemplate itself with keen skepticism. . . . We are engaged in a struggle to demonstrate our worth in a world that seems disinterested if not hostile, and we are at the same time obligated to chip away at every foundation of our enterprise. [1987:329]

Yet seven years later the same author wrote, "I think we are better off as a profession than as a priesthood, and the hallmark of a vital profession (one that is routinely recognized and adopted by others) is the diffusion into public discourse, as well as into the talk of other professions" (Chambers 1994:401).

It seems to me that anthropology can (and perhaps should) be all three—vocation, discipline, and profession: the former factor motivates us to enter this (some would say) foolhardy, rather arcane field to begin with, the middle factor makes us take seriously anthropology's long traditions and steep learning curves, and the latter factor reminds us that, after all, the general public scarcely knows what we do, good jobs *are* scarce, and we are many. (Over 10,500 of us have earned PhDs since midcentury.) But even if anthropology is still partly all three, it has yet to show that it knows how to assume its latest and most difficult role, that of an effective profession.

Derber and Schwartz call professionals "today's most powerful knowledge class," a power involving status, money, and "credentialed expertise" (1990:4–5). This professional class (also known as "mandarins" or "experts")[11] is part of the so-called *logocracy* that lays claim to that global enterprise of theory-driven, scientifically objective "rational discourse" (Derber and Schwartz 1990:28).

Is that us who are being described? What is our expertise—the culture concept? field methods? knowledge of distant others? What are our credentials—the research PhD or the increasingly common applied MA? Some of us (mostly in academia) may have some status and power? Probably few of us make serious money. Are we "theory-driven" or scientifically objective? To go back to Chambers (1987), do we anthropologists know how (and desire) to "look outward," to cultivate our "image," to expand job opportunities for our fellow graduates, to learn what (if anything) the public expects of us, and to help teach that public that we are indispensable? Does it strain credulity to compare anthropology with other "powerful" professions such as law, medicine, or architecture?

Ironically, one legacy of applied and practicing anthropology is that we have strained ever harder *to become more than simply fusty old academics:* we have wanted to enter that bigger, more turbulent realm of practical professionals jostling for contracts, connections, and the main chance. We have, as the academics may imagine, tainted ourselves with hints of political influence, impeachable ends, unpublished writings, and questionable independence.

Some have called postmodernism "an expression of exhausted progressive impulses and moral bankruptcy" (Ahmed and Shore 1995:32). Fox (1992) goes well beyond this in a sharply accusatory but persuasive piece that notes the "sheer intellectual wimpishness" and "desperation" of some contemporary anthropologists who, intimidated by the prospect of actually learning "real hard science," take refuge in "Lit Crit," vapid opinion, and the suicidal denial that anthropology can ever hope to learn anything certain about that mystical Other (Fox 1992:48,52). Fox urges us to get a grip and develop a renewed respect for the Western tradition of scientific inquiry—which "will indeed transcend local cognitive boundaries"—before it is too late and before we have totally boxed ourselves into a cozy corner of petulant irrelevance (1992:49). Singer, who calls himself an applied anthropologist subject to painful "academic craving" (surely many of us have it), writes:

> Needless to say, the whole discourse of postmodernism in anthropology privileges the doing and writing of ethnography as the very essence of anthropology's "work," while application evaporates as a component of the anthropological project: Indeed, the argument could be made that reasserting the primacy of university-based, theoretical anthropology is the hidden agenda of postmodernism within the discipline. [1995:46]

One senses much discomfort today among many anthropologists. Weiner (1995), a recent AAA president, observes that, "at present, the discipline's transitional state is fraught with discontent." She refers to anthropological "hierarchies rife with factions and jealousies," to anthropologists' well-known (to some granting agencies) inability to reach consensus, and to the field's "fractionalized stagnation" (1995:16–17). Others have noted the field's "uneasy self-criticism" (Benthall 1995:2), "an increasingly unsettled intellectual field" (Geertz 1995:13), a "loss of self-confidence" and "this paralysing uncertainty" (Ahmed and Shore 1995:15), "the sour pessimism of our own day" (Grimshaw and Hart 1995:50), and our "protracted identity crisis" (Calhoun 1992:149 fn.). Fox (1992) asserts, "The vast majority of our colleagues are intellectually lazy" (1992:51).

This dark mood has various sources, including anthropology's "loss" of the culture concept to other fields, the postmodern critique of ethnography, the de facto disintegration (often decades ago) of the "four-field" approach, and our increasingly fragmented research interests (Weiner 1995:14). It also stems from an intensified uncertainty about who "we" anthropologists (as a coherent discipline or profession) are, an uncertainty that may be even sharper among those of us working outside the university. Some inhabitants of the academy, those "unmarked (pure) academic anthropologists" (Grimshaw and Hart 1995:67), may not even be aware of this dilemma.

Conclusion

As practicing anthropologists, we need to read and think long and hard about this (and all other) new theory. But we do not have the luxury of stopping there, nor should society at large be expected to anticipate nothing more from anthropology than the clever sarcasm of postmodernism. Paredes refers to

> the crippling intellectual effects of elitist cognitive orientations in anthropology. These orientations hamper our understanding and our ability to solve the problems of a real world that bleeds, coughs, and vomits, no matter how much you "construct it." It seems sometimes that the vocational elite in anthropology are bound and determined to retreat into literary irrelevance and thereby, given their power and prestige, undercut any possibility of creating a true science of culture that might actually help to ameliorate the nasty problems of inequality, want, and overcrowding in the world. [1995:56]

We must remain thoroughly grounded (in our ethnographic forays into empirical sociocultural settings), penetrating (in our questioning and analysis), and still somehow marginal (in our disinclination to "go mainstream," to become "comfortable"). Unfortunately, as anthropology continues to try to evolve from vocation to discipline to profession, these three goals, in inverse order, have become harder to attain.

A colleague, Linda Camino, has reminded me that PhDs in anthropology today can *leave* academia with the realistic hope of securing satisfying professional careers, but it is rare that these same persons can *return* to the university to play meaningful roles. This is a serious indictment of anthropology and represents a terrible waste of human resources. Unlike other "mature" professional fields like business, medicine, law, or psychology—all of which seem to maintain a healthy respect for practitioners and require the latter to help train future MBAs, doctors, lawyers, and psychologists—anthropology persists with its heavily implicit caste/class system, in which unmarked, supposedly "normative" academicians only grudgingly respect applied or practicing colleagues. Hopefully this is changing.

Notes

1. Funding types include grants, contracts, and cooperative agreements. This chapter focuses on contracts.

2. The RFP usually consists of a formal title, identification number, and information about the due date, time, and location. There are then "Instructions, Conditions, and Notices to Offerors" as well as "Business Proposal Instructions." (The technical and business proposals must be kept quite separate, and cost information must not be mentioned in the former.) The RFP will usually state its Evaluation Criteria (e.g., the Procedural Plan is worth 45 points out of 100, Personnel/Related Experience 30 points, Management/Staffing 15 points, and Corporate Experience 10 points). The RFP typically mandates that bidders must prepare a Statement of Work (SOW) containing an Introduction, Background, Study Purposes, and Scope of Work (formal tasks to be completed). The organization of the Technical Proposal itself is usually as follows: Abstract; Table of Contents; Introduction; Procedural Plan; Management Plan and Schedule and the Performance Measurement System; Personnel; Organizational Experience; Current Contractual Obligations; Travel; Resources, Facilities, Equipment; and Subcontractors and Consultants. Attachments to the RFP may include descriptions of grantees, briefing materials, literature references, and data matrixes.

3. Many of the consultants in this site visitor pool had previously worked with CSR on another human service contract in which they had a different role: they were employed as "local ethnographers"—that is, part-time consultants who lived locally and who regularly (often over a three- to four-year period) visited, observed, and reported on their own preassigned (one project per consultant) human service projects. (See Figure 1, roles 7 and 8.) The CSAP-HRY contract attempted to reduce problems of data reliability and avoid an unwieldy number of consultants by using a smaller pool of site visitors who were regionally (not locally) based and who made only one visit to each assigned project.

4. Research firms find that federal agencies may or may not be willing to negotiate the relatively low consultant rates that are stated in RFPs. Firms like CSR are faced with a competitive disadvantage: they want to hire the best possible consultants but are sometimes unable to pay them accordingly. It is increasingly common for private consultants to charge a separate (and relatively modest) federal rate.

5. These figures are unweighted averages derived from a 1993 AAA questionnaire mailed to 325 institutions (Givens and Mahaney 1994).

6. GESO, formed in 1990, has tried to unionize Yale's humanities and social sciences graduate students and teaching assistants (TA's) (who teach ten percent of Yale's undergraduate courses). GESO, which has sought higher teaching stipends, lower health care costs, smaller class sections, and recognized procedures for complaints against the university, recently staged an unsuccessful strike that involved TA's threatening to refuse to submit grades by the official deadline (Goldin 1995; Judson 1996a). Applegate and Tulgan (1996), in a *New York Times* editorial, claim that GESO's members, facing 1990s-era grim job *realism,* have not been sympathetically received by middle-aged faculty who themselves experienced '60s-era *radicalism.* In brief, the university wants to retain graduate students (i.e., "cheap labor") "within a traditional apprenticeship system, which was set up to groom them for tenured positions that are now in short supply" (Applegate and Tulgan 1996). All of this is symptomatic of a PhD job market that has worsened since the 1989 recession, combined with the fact that there is no longer mandatory faculty retirement at age 70 (Judson 1996b).

7. Hillerman 1973, a mystery novel set on New Mexico's Zuni Indian reservation, presents Ted Isaacs, a homely archeology graduate student (self-deprecatingly described as the son of "east Tennessee white trash") who explains his "dig's" significance:

> These rocks I got here mean the rest of my life. . . . It means I get past the Ph.D. committee with no sweat, and I get the degree. And instead of being one of a hundred new Ph.D.s fighting it out for maybe three or four decent faculty places around the country, I have my pick. I have the reputation, and a book to write, and the status. And when I walk into the American Anthropological Association meetings, instead of being some grubby little pissant of a graduate assistant at some little junior college, why, I'm the man who helped fill in the missing link. It's the kind of thing that lasts you all of your life. [1973:134–135]

8. Michael Agar humorously referred to "feds, firms, and fish," the rough equivalents of my roles 9, 6, and 1 through 5, respectively (personal communication, AAA annual meeting, December 3, 1994, Atlanta, GA).

9. Clifford Geertz is skeptical that anthropology is a "discipline" at all, referring to its "blurry image," dubious theory, and "impossibly diverse" studies (from "comparative mythography to ethnobotany"). Sociocultural anthropology is, he says, "in fact rather more something one picks up as one goes along year after year" (Geertz 1995:96–97).

10. Hill (1994) contrasts two types of voluntary professional organizations: *learned societies,* which tend to have rather "impractical" academic goals and values, and *professional organizations* that focus on the economic marketplace and the protection of the practitioner's interests. LPOs, such as WAPA in Washington, DC, are examples of the latter. AAA itself is a blend of the two, although it is probably too big and diverse to be, strictly speaking, a learned society.

11. The authors identify three major United States classes today: capitalists, workers, and professionals (Derber and Schwartz 1990:19).

References Cited

Ahmed, Akbar S., and Cris N. Shore, eds.
1995 Introduction: Is Anthropology Relevant to the Contemporary World? *In* The Future of Anthropology: Its Relevance to the Contemporary World. Pp. 12–45. London: Athlone.

Applegate, Debby, and Bruce Tulgan
1996 At Yale, a Decent Life Is a Radical Idea. New York Times, January 13: 23.

Benthall, Jonathan
1995 From Self-Applause through Self-Criticism to Self-Confidence. *In* The Future of Anthropology: Its Relevance to the Contemporary World. Akbar S. Ahmed and Cris N. Shore, eds. Pp. 1–11. London: Athlone.

Calhoun, Craig
1992 Sociology, Other Disciplines, and the Project of a General Understanding of Social Life. *In* Sociology and Its Publics: The Forms and Fates of Disciplinary Organization. Terence C. Halliday and Morris Janowitz, eds. Pp. 137–195. Chicago: University of Chicago Press.

Cassell, Joan
1992 Commentary: Confessions of a Marginal Woman. Anthropology Newsletter 33(3):21, 32.

Chambers, Erve
1987 Applied Anthropology in the Post-Vietnam Era: Anticipations and Ironies. Annual Review of Anthropology 16:309–337.
1994 A World Safe for Poets. Human Organization 53(4):399–402.

Derber, Charles, and William A. Schwartz
1990 Power in the Highest Degree: Professionals and the Rise of a New Mandarin Order. New York: Oxford University Press.

Fox, Robin
1992 Anthropology and the "Teddy Bear" Picnic. Society 30(1):47–55.

Geertz, Clifford
1995 After the Fact: Two Countries, Four Decades, One Anthropologist. Cambridge, MA: Harvard University Press.

Givens, David B., and Diane Mahaney
1994 1994 Survey of Departments. Anthropology Newsletter 35(8):4–5.

Goldin, Davidson
1995 Yale Teaching Assistants Vote for a Grade Strike. New York Times, December 13: B16.

Grimshaw, Anna, and Keith Hart
1995 The Rise and Fall of Scientific Ethnography. *In* The Future of Anthropology: Its Relevance to the Contemporary World. Akbar S. Ahmed and Cris N. Shore, eds. Pp. 46–64. London: Athlone.

Halliday, Terence C.
1992 Introduction: Sociology's Fragile Professionalism. *In* Sociology and Its Publics: The Forms and Fates of Disciplinary Organization. Terence C. Halliday and Morris Janowitz, eds. Pp. 3–42. Chicago: University of Chicago Press.

Hill, Carol E.
1994 Commentary: Professional Organizations and the Future Practice of Anthropology. Practicing Anthropology 16(1):23–24.
Hillerman, Tony
1973 Dance Hall of the Dead. New York: Harper Paperbacks.
Judson, George
1996a On Deadline, Yale Students End a Strike. New York Times, January 16: B1, B4.
1996b Yale Student Strike Points to Decline in Tenured Jobs. New York Times, January 17: B6.
Kennard, Edward A., and Gordon MacGregor
1953 Applied Anthropology in Government: United States. *In* Anthropology Today: An Encyclopedic Inventory. Pp. 832–840. Chicago: University of Chicago Press.
Mead, Margaret
1973 Changing Styles of Anthropological Work. Annual Review of Anthropology 2:1–26.
Paredes, J. Anthony
1995 Notes for a Manifesto on Working-Class Anthropology. Practicing Anthropology 17(1/2):55–56.
Reed, Michael C.
1995 Institutionalizing (and Legitimizing) a System for Computer Assisted Qualitative Text Analysis. Paper presented at the 94th annual meeting of the American Anthropological Association, Washington, DC, November 19.
WAPA (Washington Association of Professional Anthropologists)
1993 Directory of Members. Washington, DC: WAPA.
1994 Directory of Members. Washington, DC: WAPA.
1995 Directory of Members. Washington, DC: WAPA.
Webster, Cynthia M., and Michael L. Burton
1992 Summary Report on the Academic Employment of Women in Anthropology. Anthropology Newsletter 33(2):1,21,23.
Weiner, Annette B.
1995 Culture and Our Discontents. American Anthropologist 97:14–21.

"That Is Not My Role, Really": Hazards in Entering the Field and Developing a Role in Contract Research

Margaret McKenna

The anthropologist who does contract research, either occasionally or as part of a regular livelihood, often encounters role uncertainties and ambiguous normative expectations and thereby ventures into uncharted territory. Time pressures, the distinctive nature of the activities performed, and the work context all contribute to the occupational hazards and role-related dilemmas of the contract ethnographer.[1]

When doing such short-term research, the anthropologist might be advised to develop the personal attributes that Martin Luther King Jr. (1969:16) sought in his supporters. He exhorted them to have "a tough mind and a tender heart" and to demonstrate "incisive thinking, realistic appraisal, and decisive judgment." The contract ethnographer, who is often asked to assess human service program impacts and judge how well these projects fit their targeted communities, is also called upon to think incisively, appraise realistically, and judge decisively, this after being rather abruptly cast into a sea of project participants, project staff members, and community representatives.

In such a research context, the contract ethnographer is challenged to define, establish, and develop a professional role. This role includes functional elements that have been previously alluded to (i.e., assessment, appraisal, and judgment) but also involves other contextual dimensions with professional and practical implications. The starting point here is neither the ethical debate about the performance of research activity (Fetterman 1984) nor the debates contrasting applied and basic research (Chambers 1989) or applied and theoretical anthropology (Foster 1969). Rather, the starting point is a discussion of the various dimensions of the contract ethnographer's role.

It is true that a well-trained nonanthropologist could also carry out the tasks performed by a contract ethnographer. Nevertheless, by virtue of methodological training in naturalistic inquiry, inductive analysis, holistic perspective, and a comparative framework, the anthropologist is especially well prepared to serve as a contract ethnographer. Anthropologists trained in qualitative research and long-term fieldwork have proven to be adept at applying those research approaches.

Functional and Contextual Dimensions of the Contract Ethnographer's Role

There are three functional and contextual dimensions that place the contract ethnographer in a unique position: (1) the nature of the research (i.e., intensive and brief in an obligatory relationship with a primary stakeholder); (2) the congruence and the deviation of the ethnographer's role from that of other practicing anthropologists; and (3) the role ambiguities that arise from attempting to meet (and negotiate) multiple expectations. The stakes are high, and the contract ethnographer is under pressure to produce results in a short time. The contract ethnographer must meet the demands of the stakeholders, including the funding agency and the grantee, while still trying to satisfy her or his own professional standards, all of this in the face of an unclear role.

The Nature of the Research

Contract ethnography is, by design, stripped of the extended time frame that allows traditional ethnography to engage in theoretical debate and development. The contract ethnographer's challenge is to assess, analyze, and consolidate data in a report that may stand alone or be integrated with other documentation. The inevitable time constraints induce several tensions including concurrent work obligations, rapid immersion into the field, and the shortcomings of trying to work with a folk expert(s) while efficiently identifying meaningful data sources.

One source of role tension stems from the ethnographer having to perform several research activities at the same time: for example, reading agency documents and records, interviewing key informants, planning and conducting group interviews, and mapping the local neighborhood. Time on site may be consumed by such work, and it is possible that only after leaving the site is the ethnographer able to reflect on what information was acquired and what were the meaningful interactions that warrant being analyzed. While on site, the contract ethnographer rarely has any time away from the data, that is, a break that would provide the opportunity to analyze and reflect upon data gathered from informants.

The anthropologist conducting traditional, long-term research usually has sufficient time to go through stages of gaining entry and acceptance among the individuals to be studied. In contract research, however, the ethnographer has to rapidly enter and leave the world of project participants, project staff, and community agency directors. Rapid changes in research approaches and styles are sometimes required in order to collect data from street informants, local government leaders, project managers, and frontline social service providers. As Pelto states, "In most cases, the fieldworker encounters social complexities and problems at every turn, and successful role maintenance demands great presence of mind, flexibility, and luck" (1970:200).

In order to develop role clarity, the contract ethnographer may have to explain what an ethnographer does to overcome a local misperception that he or she is an evaluator. Project staff may reasonably expect that an evaluator will provide constructive feedback or serve as an expert on a given intervention or in the specific curricula employed in the projects. But the contract ethnographer is often neither a good source of immediate feedback nor an expert. The ethnographer, who typically was not intended to be a technical adviser, tries to refrain from making comments that could be construed as advice so as to minimize his or her influence upon (or "contamination" of) a project. If misperceived as an evaluator—that is, someone who is looking for deficiencies to correct—the ethnographer may find that prospective informants stop talking for fear of disclosing information damaging to themselves or the project.

The ethnographer may also encounter resistance from project staff or agency representatives who are well versed in standard quantitative research methods. They may doubt that any reliable product will come from the ethnographer's qualitative efforts and may therefore even delay providing needed information.

In an effort to understand the local culture, the ethnographer may seek out a local "folk expert," an individual whom outsiders identify as a leading authority on a community's culture (Bell and Jankowiak 1992:413). This expert may, for example, be an educator or a service provider who, although originally from outside the local community, may have become conversant with the local culture and political climate. While a folk expert may help the ethnographer understand the local community, this relationship may also spark clashes over differing role expectations and statuses and disagreements over the interpretation of data.[2] The folk expert's possible role as community advocate may cause the expert to hamper the contract ethnographer's collection of sufficient information to generate a realistic or representative report.

Furthermore, the ethnographer's distinctive professional preparation and ability to frame the analysis contextually and theoretically (both desirable skills to the funding stakeholder) may be threatening to the folk expert. If the folk expert responds by offering a competing analysis, the ethnographer may become enmeshed in time-consuming debates to reaffirm the purpose and strategy of the ethnographic work.

To reduce such potential conflicts, the contract ethnographer must seek out key informants representing a range of constituencies essential to understanding the local culture. Ideally, these informants do not seek to establish themselves as local authorities and will therefore willingly clarify the local context. The contract ethnographer who seeks out and reads local newspapers, neighborhood newsletters, or meeting notices may in this way gain sufficient information to identify appropriate, approachable key informants. The challenge is to select one's informants carefully and quickly to optimize data collection while simultaneously listening to the voices of persons in varied roles and positions.

Congruence and Deviation of the Contract Ethnographer's Role from that of the Practicing Anthropologist

The contract ethnographer's several role constraints distinguish the role from that of practicing anthropologists. These constraints include: (1) engaging in research that has policy implications—but then being required to relinquish the data without being able to translate them into policy; (2) researching issues identified by someone else (a stakeholder); and (3) working in an asymmetrical, unreciprocated relationship with informants. These constraints are discussed below.

Research with Frustrated Policy Implications. The contract ethnographer's primary task is researching issues of contemporary social or political concern in order to contribute to the knowledge base and perhaps inform public debate (Firth 1981). The practicing anthropologist is defined by a complex of research-based, instrumental activities that produce socially desired change or stability in specific cultural systems through the provision of information, the formulation of policy, and/or the initiation of direct action (van Willigen 1984:277). The contract ethnographer differs from the practicing anthropologist because the contract ethnographer's focus is on researching issues known to be of interest to policy makers or other potential users while not actually engaging in policy making (Mair 1984).[3]

Nevertheless, one aspect of the contract ethnographer's role closely approximates that of a practicing anthropologist: both focus on practical rather than theoretical arguments. A practicing anthropologist is defined as "a professionally trained individual who applies specialized knowledge, skills and experience to problem solving in any of the human dimensions (past, present, and future)" (NAPA 1990). Contract ethnographers—like applied anthropologists—also often have a knowledge base of specialized skills to bring to problem solving. According to Foster, applied anthropologists "could describe their professional activities in programs that have as their primary goals changes in human behavior believed *to ameliorate contemporary social, economic, and technological problems,* rather than the development of social and cultural theory" (1969:54, emphasis added).

But it is precisely in the *application of skills to problem solving* that the role of the contract ethnographer deviates from that of the practicing or applied anthropologist. The contract ethnographer is often deterred from directly applying skills toward problem resolution and is confined to describing the problem as the basis for subsequent intervention designed and implemented by other parties. The contract ethnographer stands apart from what Sol Tax called an "action" anthropologist because the latter usually assumes the coordinated goals of carrying out scientific inquiry on social organization and social dynamics while also identifying solutions to resolve a group's situations (Tax 1952).[4]

The contract ethnographer's role is thus substantially more constrained than that of the practicing anthropologist, who may apply accumulated research experience and knowledge toward the development of programmatic policies. The contract ethnographer, especially when working on short assignments or on multisite projects, usually produces information in a descriptive, analytical report. Such reports often support recommendations that are generally to be finalized and implemented *by others*. Such reports often discuss multiple factors relevant to solving problems, developing policy, revising programs, or identifying alternative solutions.

The contract ethnographer, who may be one of several ethnographers working at different sites, is expected to relinquish the tasks of interpreting and translating analysis into program policy and practice. He or she usually submits reports to a nonanthropologist (often employed at an agency level) who is responsible for policy formation, program development, and/or program assessment and evaluation.

The contract ethnographer's report is, once again, intended to communicate findings to the managers, policy analysts, and program developers who may transform the findings into policy or program development. The contract ethnographer needs to recognize that all of these readers have their own ideologies that will influence their interpretations of the data. This fact challenges the contract ethnographer to prepare an account that will be acceptable to multiple readers/stakeholders. The contract ethnographer aims to translate the values and ideologies of the informants, the project, and the community to the funding agency while recognizing that agency's ideological predisposition. This role constraint is so important that the title and role expectation of contract anthropologist should be reevaluated in favor of a broader notion of a contextually defined role (Grillo 1985).

An Asymmetrical Relationship. The social and political issues confronting the contract ethnographer usually fit the research agenda of a "customer," that is, a primary stakeholder, such as a federal or state agency. The contract ethnographer, who undertakes problem-oriented research requested by this customer, then usually provides a "deliverable" (report) by a certain date. When the primary stakeholder is a federal agency or other public entity, the ethnographer learns to become compliant with the particular rules and parameters of that stakeholder's interests, study design, and time frame. McNabb (1993:218) describes such contractual arrangements as complicating factors that enforce performance and the delivery of services under threat of sanction: the client can terminate the contract or bring a lawsuit if the anthropologist does not produce.

The supply-and-demand relationship with the stakeholder leaves little opportunity for the contract ethnographer to drop one topic of inquiry in favor of another or to function as an advocate for the studied group. The contract ethnographer may be obliged to focus on a preordained analytical framework in order to accumulate the data for cross-site comparisons or program evaluation. There is rarely time to develop the kinds of reciprocal exchanges of information or services (with the project participants, service delivery staff, or administrative team members) that would be afforded an anthropologist conducting long-term research. The short time allocated for the data collection and analysis forces the ethnographer into a whirlwind of "must-see" activities with little time for observation, participation, or rapport building.

The contract ethnographer, unlike an applied or practicing anthropologist, does not assume the role of culture broker or ombudsperson. The practicing anthropologist, for example, might serve as an advocate to assist local community members in receiving benefits to which they are entitled (Kuhlmann 1992). While the contract ethnographer may be proficient at conducting research of benefit to the community, time is allocated only for collecting ethnographic data from informants; this fact sustains the asymmetrical researcher-informant relationship.

The contract ethnographer often does not even have the opportunity to nurture relationships with community members to support their self-advocacy. Whereas an anthropologist conducting more traditional research has ethical and moral obligations to the local community and to the scientific community (Rubenstein 1986), the contract ethnographer seems to remain largely disengaged from interaction with the local or scientific community. The contract ethnographer may feel an allegiance to community informants, but he or she is also responsible to the bureaucratic stakeholder and the funding agency.

The contract ethnographer's primary responsibility is to submit a report to the stakeholder, and he or she may not be required (or even allowed) to submit that report to personnel in the project that was studied. Government agencies often require that descriptive or analytical information not be sent to the local project staff until after the funding agency has reviewed the report. This delayed transmission of information further reinforces the asymmetrical nature of the relationship between the researcher and informants.

Whether feedback to the community is provided or not, the community is changed by a contract ethnographer's visit. To adapt a tenet of interpretive anthropology, the description and characterization of project participants and agency personnel are forms of intervention in their lives (Johannsen 1992). The programmatic impact of the contract ethnographer's description may be more subtle and more delayed than the immediate efforts of practicing anthropologists (who make their presence more obviously and intentionally felt), but it will be felt.

In this volume, Gladys Levis-Pilz describes the unexpected impact at one study site resulting from project staff members reading her report. As far as I know, in this particular federal contract most site-visitor reports did not spark this degree of controversy. Perhaps there was less controversy because the contract ethnographers were involved in the local scene only briefly and were party to only limited disclosure of sensitive material. Nevertheless, most ethnographers were indeed aware that their mere presence on site might be recognized as an intervention or even as an intrusion.

Role Acceptance: Multiple Expectations

Despite the frequent necessity of offering a delayed report to the local grantee agency and of being constrained from providing direct local assistance, the contract ethnographer does often believe that his or her efforts fulfill a purpose, that is to say, they provide information that may shape policy, program development, or the initiation of direct action. There is thus at least one primary product of the contract ethnographer—information—that may be associated with policy and action. The contract ethnographer is not merely the transmitter of information but is also observer, assessor, appraiser, judge, and interpreter. The contract ethnographer's responsibility is to produce a valid and reliable account of reality (van Willigen 1984:281).

The contract ethnographer is concerned with collecting information; he or she does not merely identify independent variables but describes the actual or potential interactions and relationships between these variables. He or she aims to describe the relationships between the observed activities, to describe how they are amenable to change, and to identify potential change agents. For example, the contract ethnographer can readily assess the relationship between repeated academic failure and a decision to drop out of school. If the studied project is in a position to affect academic failure, then the focus shifts to describing how that change is implemented. The contract ethnographer has the additional burden of moving beyond the traditional examination and analysis of the relationships between social group members (or key factors) in order to examine a project in its entirety.

The transmission of information becomes problematic for the contract ethnographer if the report involves unexpected findings, seems counterintuitive, or is perceived as undesirable (McNabb 1993:218). The contract ethnographer's knowledge may be hazardous to his or her livelihood since he or she treats informants, the stakeholders themselves, as well as the linkages and relationships that are established between a grantee agency and a funding agency, as subjects for inquiry. What the contract ethnographer is capable of doing is disclosing facts or developing interpretations that may challenge the assumptions of report recipients (Grillo 1985).

The ethnographic report may "challenge what others want to believe" (Colson 1985), which may leave informants and clients disinterested in hearing the results or inclined to reject the report. This is especially possible when there has been a change in a social service project's management or when project personnel changes occur between the time of the contract ethnographer's visit and the time that the grantee agency finally sees the report. The contract ethnographer's portrayal of a project at a certain point in time may be extremely useful to that stakeholder to document project development and to underscore prerequisites for project growth and maturity. But this relevance may be lost on project staff who only learn about it long after they have moved on to new challenges.

The Development of Role Acceptance: Role Negotiation

The constraints of the contract ethnographer's role require that person to explain and negotiate what he or she actually does in light of what she or he does *not* do (i.e., develop policy, revise programs, provide immediate feedback). The contract ethnographer enters the field as a gatherer and purveyor of information. As such, the role is descriptive, but it lacks prescriptive or instrumental functions.

The contract ethnographer conducts interviews with informants at different hierarchical or functional levels in an agency, facility, or project in order to clarify roles, expectations, and anticipated relationships among these informants. The contract ethnographer may have to use diplomatic communication skills in order to effectively interview many informants in a short period. He or she must appear receptive to many viewpoints without being perceived as being aligned with any particular community leader, project staff members, or local organizer. Yet in the course of speaking with key informants, the contract ethnographer may (perhaps inadvertently) reconcile, redirect, or even intensify the conflicting expectations that the sponsor stakeholder, the agency, or the project may have regarding the contract ethnographer's role.

The contract ethnographer is clearly at the heart of this unique relationship that is neither the traditional dyadic relationship between anthropologist and studied community nor the triadic relationship of anthropologist, community, and funding agency. The contract ethnographer really represents a cornerstone in a quadratic relationship involving him or herself, the community, the grantee agency, and the agency requesting the report. Both the studied community and the local grantee agency may rightly perceive themselves as under scrutiny by the sponsoring agency. The contract ethnographer thus serves as the intermediary between what has been termed the "decision makers" and the "decision takers"; that is to say, those who make policy and those who receive its outcomes. The ethnographer moves back and forth between these two worlds.

The contract ethnographer's motto could readily become "Offend no one." The contract ethnographer learns early not to take sides in community issues but to work instead to collect information from all the actors, including project participants, line staff, administrative team members, school district personnel, community agency directors, and neighborhood informants. The contract ethnographer's dilemma is to weigh the information received from very willing informants while also trying to obtain information from reluctant ones in order to arrive at a balanced appraisal.

Taking this neutral position assumes that the contract ethnographer can function as a neutral observer. It leaves little room or time for disclosing or dealing with conflicts of interest, as when agencies are competing for limited resources or social recognition. The neutrality imposed upon the contract ethnographer may even preclude full interaction with the principal group in which one is interested; for example, the grantee agency or a competing community faction (Jacobs 1974:209). The neutral status and the elevation of the contract ethnographer to the position of observer actually creates some confusion among the very people with whom the ethnographer is interacting. Members of our society have been socialized to identify and respond to others primarily based upon their perceived statuses and political positions. The preservation of neutrality creates an ambivalent and ambiguous role for the contract ethnographer and a resultingly subtle interpersonal tension (Kimball 1972). The very virtues of anthropology—the culturally relativist stance and the resistance to making conclusions that could jeopardize one's objective position—are what lead to criticism.

The contract ethnographer is often challenged to convince stakeholders, including the community and the sponsors, of the legitimacy of qualitative data (collected by traditional anthropological methods) in contrast to survey data. The contract ethnographer may have to compromise on the use of some traditional anthropological methods in favor of the more rapid administration of questionnaires and group interviews in order to obtain comparative data.

There are further restraints on the definition of the problem area under investigation and on the dissemination of findings (Grillo 1985). One is the professional concern that the intricate relationships and the description of the factors that have produced these relationships should neither be reduced to mere words nor lost entirely. It is of paramount interest to the contract ethnographer that the context be understood, but it is equally vital to a nonanthropologist engaged in program planning or policy development to capture other data in a report. A related tension concerns the contract ethnographer's desire to share the richness of the data while being forced to play a waiting game until reports have been submitted and reviewed by all the agencies involved.

Conclusion

The dilemmas associated with the role of a contract ethnographer include those incurred while (1) entering the field, (2) performing various functions, and (3) negotiating a role that allows the production of a research report. The contract ethnographer confronts the dilemma of being the producer of an information-bearing report who nevertheless is not in control of the product's end use (Grillo 1985). This is neither an excuse nor a defense but is evidence of the contract ethnographer's frustration at not being able to retain any sense of possession of the report. Nevertheless, the contract ethnographer's report, if it embodies incisive thinking and realistic appraisal, will likely have a positive impact, what Belshaw refers to as the application of anthropological knowledge that will mitigate the bad and enhance the good (1976:257). The outcomes associated with the review of a report and the subsequent implementation of report recommendations could result in desirable programmatic changes.

Several key role issues have emerged here. The contract ethnographer's role deviates from the functions of many practicing anthropologists. This role is determined by contextual dimensions that include the differing ideological realities that must be assessed by the ethnographer. The contract ethnographer stands apart from the practicing anthropologist, who may focus his or her skills on intentional intervention.

Contract ethnography does, however, bear some resemblance to some tenets of so-called postmodernist ethnography. The contract ethnographer, like the postmodern ethnographer, aims to develop and present an effective dialogue that will simultaneously satisfy the ethnographer, the informant, and the stakeholder. The contract ethnographer is unlikely to achieve fully such a reciprocal exchange of authority and expertise with informants (which would truly be indicative of a postmodernist ethnography) (Johannsen 1992). Nevertheless, the contract ethnographer, by virtue of his or her obligatory relationship with the funding agency and the respect that is granted him or her as a result of that relationship, is likely to be credited, rightly or not, with some authority and expertise.

As if influenced by postmodernist ethnography, the contract ethnographer does, however, pursue the goals of enlightening various readerships in order to produce greater understanding among both the people of a selected community or project as well as the outsiders who are interested in them (Johannsen 1992). He or she does provide the structure for the members of a community, informants in a project, agency staff, and other informants to convey their cultural representations. The contract ethnographer does apply specialized skills and methods to describe and analyze community information, values, and ideology in reports that are to be read by decision and policy makers. In other words, the product will most likely be used (or intentionally not used) by other individuals in either formulating policies and in implementing change or in maintaining stability in social systems.

Notes

1. See the introduction to this volume for a discussion of how this role fits into the academic, applied, and practicing anthropology taxonomy.

2. For a discussion of the role of the folk expert, including case studies of role conflicts with anthropologists, see Bell and Jankowiak 1992.

3. Foster (1969) refers to the social structural context of applied and theoretical anthropology without discussing the nonresearch activities of the applied anthropologist. In

1984 van Willigen differentiated three products of the applied anthropologist in the domains of information, policy, and action. He further stated that the anthropologist usually furnishes information to a nonanthropological information consumer responsible for policy formulation (1984:278). In the last decade, anthropologists have been more involved in action and policy (e.g., rural development projects, health, and education [Gow 1995]).

4. While practicing anthropologists may not totally subscribe to the tenets of action anthropology, many acknowledge the gains made by the development of action anthropology four decades ago and are also inclined toward the practical application of inquiry. The contract ethnographer stands apart from many practicing anthropologists who, owing to their traditions in action anthropology, would take on problem resolution following scientific inquiry. The ethnographer working under contract has neither the time nor the authorization to engage in problem resolution.

References Cited

Bell, James, and William R. Jankowiak
1992 The Ethnographer vs. the Folk Expert: Pitfalls of Contract Ethnography. Human Organization 51:412–417.
Belshaw, Cyril
1976 The Sorcerer's Apprentice: An Anthropology of Public Policy. New York: Pergamon Press.
Chambers, Erve
1989 Applied Anthropology: A Practical Guide. Prospect Heights, IL: Waveland.
Colson, Elizabeth
1985 Using Anthropology in a World on the Move. Human Organization 44:191–196.
Fetterman, David M., ed.
1984 Guilty Knowledge, Dirty Hands, and other Ethical Dilemmas. *In* Ethnography in Educational Evaluation. Pp. 211–235. Beverly Hills, CA: Sage Publications.
Firth, Raymond
1981 Engagement and Detachment: Reflections on Applying Social Anthropology to Social Affairs. Human Organization 40:193–201.
Foster, George M.
1969 Applied Anthropology. Boston: Little, Brown.
Gow, David D.
1995 Anthropology, the Environment, and the Third World: Principles, Power, and Practice. *In* Global Ecosystems: Creating Options through Anthropological Perspectives. NAPA Bulletin, 15. P. J. Puntenney, ed. Pp. 46–59. Arlington, VA: American Anthropological Association.
Grillo, Ralph
1985 Applied Anthropology in the 1980s: Retrospect and Prospect. *In* Social Anthropology and Development Policy. Ralph Grillo and Alan Rew, eds. Pp. 1–36. London: Tavistock.
Jacobs, Sue-Ellen
1974 Action and Advocacy Anthropology. Human Organization 33:209–215.
Johannsen, Agneta M.
1992 Applied Anthropology and Post-Modernist Ethnography. Human Organization 51:71–81.
Kimball, Solon T.
1972 Learning a New Culture. *In* Crossing Cultural Boundaries: The Anthropological Experience. Solon T. Kimball and James B. Watson, eds. Pp. 48–62. Newbury Park, CA: Sage Publications.
King, Martin Luther, Jr.
1969 Strength to Love. London: Fontana.
Kuhlmann, Annette
1992 Collaborative Research among the Kickapoo Tribe of Oklahoma. Human Organization 51:274–283.
McNabb, Steven
1993 Contract and Consulting Anthropology in Alaska. Human Organization 52: 216–224.

Mair, Lucy
1984 Anthropology and Development. London: Macmillan.
NAPA (National Association for the Practice of Anthropology)
1990 Membership Information. Brochure. Washington, DC: American Anthropological Association.
Pelto, Pertti J.
1970 Anthropological Research: The Structure of Inquiry. New York: Harper and Row.
Rubenstein, Robert A.
1986 Reflections on Action Anthropology: Some Developmental Dynamics of an Anthropological Tradition. Human Organization 45:270–279.
Tax, Sol
1952 Action Anthropology. America Indigenia 12:103–109.
van Willigen, John
1984 Truth and Effectiveness: An Essay on the Relationships between Information, Policy and Action in Applied Anthropology. Human Organization 43:277–282.

What Can Anthropologists Offer Ethnographic Program Evaluation?

Linda A. Camino

> [I]f you want to understand what a science is, you should look in the first instance not at its theories or its findings, and certainly not at what its apologists say about it; you should look at what the practitioners of it do . . . in anthropology, or anyway social anthropology, what the practitioners do is ethnography. . . . From one point of view, that of the textbook, doing ethnography is establishing rapport, selecting informants, transcribing texts, taking genealogies, mapping fields, keeping a diary, and so on. But it is not these things, techniques and received procedures, that define the enterprise. What defines it is the kind of intellectual effort it is.
>
> —Clifford Geertz 1973:5–6

It is perhaps unsporting to quote Geertz in abbreviated form. In many forums, he has succinctly and gracefully articulated the nature of the anthropological enterprise. But the purpose of highlighting the above words is to emphasize that the persistent dichotomy drawn between academic and applied, or scholarly and practicing, anthropology masks an essential reality: that anthropology and ethnography are inevitably intertwined no matter where the anthropologist is doing ethnography and what the nature of the ethnographic pursuit. The recurring call for ethnography to serve both within and without the anthropological community as a vantage point from which to understand contemporary life is, in effect, a mandate for infusing our knowledge and talents both into the intellectual record and into humanitarian social policies.

If ethnography represents the essence of the anthropological spirit, it is an inherently ambiguous representation. It has been cast, for example, as methodologies (Miles and Huberman 1994), ways of shaping observations (Edgerton and Langness 1974), texts (Clifford and Marcus 1986; Marcus and Cushman 1987), epistemological interpretation (Geertz 1973), and process as well as product (Agar 1980, 1986). Ethnography has also clearly captured the research imagination of many disciplines and professions such as sociology,[1] education, psychology, nursing, and social work.

Ethnography has been increasingly used in program evaluation. Patton (1990) states that evaluation:

> include[s] any effort to increase human effectiveness through systematic data-based inquiry. Human beings are engaged in all kinds of efforts to make the world a better place. . . . In these and other efforts . . . the question of whether the people involved are accomplishing what they want to accomplish

> arises. When one examines and judges accomplishments and effectiveness, one is engaged in evaluation. When this examination of effectiveness is conducted systematically and empirically through careful data collection and thoughtful analysis, one is engaged in evaluation *research*. [1990:11]

Much has been written about the proliferation of qualitative evaluation research since the 1960s, during which time ethnography has steadily received more attention.[2] Indeed, the term *ethnography* has diffused into the evaluation lexicon and is now widely employed in requests for proposals (RFPs), contracts, conference presentations, spoken language, and even, albeit more rarely, job want ads.

Yet this discourse makes apparent that there are both anthropological and nonanthropological kinds of ethnography.[3] As such, several questions arise: How do anthropologists and nonanthropologists construe ethnography and its place in evaluation research? More practically, is there any value that anthropological training brings to ethnography as used in evaluation? If so, what is the nature of this "value added" and how can it be expressed to sponsors of such research?

Before addressing these questions, I point out some broad similarities between practitioners of classic ethnography and qualitative evaluation researchers. First, both seek grounded knowledge: the ethnographer and the evaluation researcher gather firsthand knowledge about peoples' lives and meanings. Second, both are engaged in a scientific as well as an artistic endeavor. (Just as there are ethnographers who adhere more to either "objective" science or "subjective" humanities, so are there evaluators with comparable preferences.) Third, both are required to protect the ethical rights of all stakeholders. Fourth, both realize that "truth" is (to borrow a phrase from Van Maanen [1995]) a "many splintered—however splendored thing" (1995:12), reflected and refracted through numerous stakeholder contexts. Fifth, both are cognizant of the political realities (i.e., human activity implies conflict over power, status, and resource distribution) that permeate their enterprises.

These parallels between ethnography and qualitative evaluation bespeak their affinity for one another. Although "ethnographic" and "qualitative" evaluation research are becoming fused in the sphere of contract research, the task remains to articulate the special nature of anthropological ethnography.

Thinking Ethnographically about Evaluation Research

For the purposes of this chapter, I perused several recent texts in qualitative and evaluation research to see how ethnography was discussed. I also interviewed ten PhD-level practitioners of ethnographic program evaluation (all of whom have worked on federal contracts, and several on the contract discussed in this volume) using a schedule of ten open-ended questions, such as:

> How do you define or describe ethnography? What relation does ethnography hold to qualitative research? What is useful about using ethnography in program evaluation? What is not useful? What are the distinctive features of an evaluation report you write based on ethnographic research? Can anyone do ethnography? What do you need in order to be a good ethnographic evaluation researcher?

Five respondents were trained as anthropologists and the other five in other disciplines (including education, psychology, and social work). On average, interviews lasted between one and two hours. In addition, this essay draws upon my experience in conducting various program evaluations over the past six years.

Ethnographic Evaluation Research Literature

In this literature, ethnography generally tends to be equated with concepts such as "case study," "participant observation," "rich description," "open-ended" or "in-depth interviewing," "focus group interviews," and "naturalistic" approaches (Lincoln and Guba 1985; Miles and Huberman 1994; Scriven 1993; Strauss and Corbin 1990; Yin 1984). Patton 1990 and Pittman and Maxwell 1992 contain sections discussing the anthropological roots of ethnography and its relationship to phenomenology, hermeneutical inquiry, ethnomethodology, and symbolic interactionism. They also review how ethnography has increasingly become an approach to understanding institutional and organizational culture. Wolcott (1992:23) and Miles and Huberman (1994:6–7) present diagrams that map ethnography's relationship to other forms of qualitative research and that clarify that ethnography is but one of numerous types of qualitative research.

Wolcott emphasizes that what makes ethnography distinctive is "a sense of structure for conducting fieldwork and a commitment to cultural interpretation . . . if cultural analysis is not your goal, then ethnography is a misnomer, although you may draw upon ethnographic *techniques* in conducting your fieldwork" (1995:108). Agar similarly distinguishes between conducting a full-scale ethnography and a study that is ethnographic. He believes that one can employ key elements of ethnographic research using ethnographic assumptions but that this is best described as "qualitative," not "ethnographic," work (1993:12–13).

Two general observations derive from the above works. First, "qualitative," "ethnographic," and "ethnography" do not admit to easy parsing. Second, in trying to apprehend ethnography it is not easy to separate its techniques from its guiding epistemologies.

Interview Results

Three major themes distinguished the views of the five anthropologists interviewed from those of the five professionals who were not trained as anthropologists:[4]

Theme 1: Anthropologists spoke of ethnography as a process that includes the written narrative generated by the inquiry.

All anthropologists and nonanthropologists understood ethnography as context-based description, emphasizing entering the field with minimal preconceived categories and a discrete set of methods. But three of the five anthropologists also defined ethnography as the written account itself. That none of the nonanthropologists used this definition suggests that such texts may not be as salient to their interests, needs, training, or professional orientations. In fact, throughout their responses to most of the questions, these same three anthropologists continually referred to such written products, affirming, for example, the need to include direct quotations and local language in reports, to incorporate theoretical points that go beyond individual case conclusions, and to avoid writing "badly," "dully," "opaquely," or in "jargon." Given anthropology's cross-cultural deciphering and decoding aims that make translation and interpretation so important, it is not surprising that written texts are essential for anthropologists.

Theme 2: Anthropologists (unlike any of the nonanthropologists) cited the importance of their disciplinary background in pursuing ethnographic endeavors.

All five anthropologists held that "the anthropological perspective" makes possible "good" ethnography. According to them, two dimensions of this perspective are fundamental: holism and a comparative stance. Anthropologists believed that holism allows them not only to examine microcontexts empirically but also to determine more abstractly how the descriptions of the various contexts fit together into a big picture. In fact, three anthropologists noted that they had been commended by evaluation sponsors on their ability to unify seemingly contradictory and fragmentary pieces of information into a coherent storyline that was both grounded in the data and that "rang true" for diverse stakeholders.

Holism was also discussed in concert with the ethnographic method of participant observation, a method not mentioned in any of the responses of the nonanthropologists. Participant observation was described, for example, as "trying to immerse yourself as much as possible in a program or community," "not just visiting a particular program and looking at what the directors want to show you, but looking further," "eating in restaurants close to the program," "visiting local businesses," "attending community events program participants attend," or "doing some shopping where program participants do theirs."

The words of one anthropologist respondent captured the gist of all the anthropologists' comments in describing the importance of anthropology's comparative stance:

> Anthropology was born as a comparative discipline. . . . These comparisons help you see what's really worth pursuing, and help you in avoiding spurious

> conclusions. . . . Comparison helps you look for overall patterns, and recognize the ones that are not really important.

Studying anthropological history, theory, and ethnographic texts, four anthropologists affirmed, also provides a comparative framework that aids in cultivating reflexive and critical thinking skills. They stated that these efforts encourage anthropologists to view skeptically "universal" explanations about human behavior and illuminate the inequalities of race, class, gender, and other power relationships so that such discourses are deconstructed.

Theme 3: Anthropologists noted the salience of extended fieldwork in preparing them to be good ethnographers.

According to all ten of the anthropologists and nonanthropologists, one's ability to do ethnography involves both natural talent and technical skills. Natural talent was thought to include, for example: "liking people," "patience," "tolerance for ambiguity," "willingness to make mistakes," and "willingness to assume a posture of learning" (as opposed to being the "expert"). Technical skills cited included "listening," "observing," "interviewing," "seeing patterns," and "drawing conclusions." Interestingly, all agreed that no one could become a good ethnographer unless he or she first possessed some natural talent—that is to say, training can develop these talents, but cannot substitute for them.

But while three nonanthropologists thought that short periods of ethnographic research could adequately constitute part of their training and development in carrying out ethnographic research, four anthropologists concurred that it was their initial doctoral fieldwork experience, conducted continuously over an extended time period, that ineluctably perfected the capability to "look," "listen," "identify relevant data," "record data," and "figure out complex patterns." They said that this experience gives one a full repertoire of skills—not just in the sense of research techniques, but in wisdom as well—and significantly prepares the ethnographer for briefer research situations.

Implications of the Interview Data

Throughout the interviews, four of the five anthropologists lamented that employers and clients rarely understand the significance of an advanced anthropology degree, while the gloss "qualitative" (and more recently "ethnographic") research experience impresses people. They said that potential employers usually have little idea how the in-depth "field experience" benefits ethnographic research. Two anthropologists mused that any researcher with a qualitative bent could label him or herself as an "ethnographer" and sponsors would accept it at face value. This may be due to a prevailing view that virtually anyone can use "nonrigorous, qualitative" methods. But as Patton points out,

> The simple fact that a person is equipped with functioning senses does not make that person a skilled observer . . . training includes learning how to write descriptively; practicing the disciplined recording of field notes; knowing how to separate detail from trivia in order to achieve the former without being overwhelmed by the latter; and using rigorous methods to validate observations. Training researchers to become astute and skilled observers is particularly difficult because so many people think that they are "natural" observers and, therefore, have very little to learn. [1990:201]

Because of these preconceptions, anthropologists face two challenges. First, we need to reflect on ways in which our disciplinary background, including the extended field experience, offers training in these deceptively simple methods. We then need to formulate explicit ways of conceptualizing and talking about how our background and training, including our intellectual orientation as well as methodology, can benefit the concerns of contract research sponsors.

The rest of this chapter takes a modest step in taking up these challenges. It should be noted that McKenna (see her chapter) discusses the role distinctions between "contract ethnographers," "evaluators," and "practicing anthropologists." If I read her correctly, the contract ethnographer (a role that I have assumed in the past) essentially provides descriptive, contextualized information about a project or program and is rarely, if ever, empowered to make recommendations for problem solving or to influence decision making, both of which constitute the domain of practicing anthropologists or evaluators.

Since McKenna has already thoroughly described the contract ethnographer role, I wish to address the role of what I will call the "ethnographic evaluator." While contract ethnographers may be hired essentially just to *describe* or *document* some portion of a larger evaluation effort, ethnographic evaluators are, by contrast, more integrally involved in the overall evaluation effort, including research design, protocol construction, data gathering, analysis, interpretation, and providing constructive feedback to stakeholders. I hope in this chapter to bring home the notion that anthropologists, by virtue of our background training and skills, are well suited to assume the more ambitious role of ethnographic evaluator, not just the descriptive role of contract ethnographer.

My discussion employs several assumptions regarding qualitative evaluation and ethnographic research: (1) both are open-ended systems for inquiry; (2) both are dynamic processes; (3) both require flexible strategy shifts as situations change; and (4) both are *interpretive* enterprises in which the researchers' views are refracted through their individual human lenses.

I also argue that anthropologists possess several preadaptive traits that prepare us to conduct ethnographic evaluation. The term *preadaptive*, borrowed from evolutionary theory, refers to a characteristic, originally acquired as an adaptation to a specialized econiche, that proves also to be advantageous in new circumstances. Below I consider five areas of preadaptive anthropological knowledge and experience: approach, ethnographic methodology, data handling, presentation of results, and working with stakeholders. The focus is practical and aims to stimulate anthropologists to think explicitly about the benefits that our anthropological training can bring to the conduct of program evaluation.

Approach

It is often assumed that the "ethnographic" part of evaluation exclusively involves visits to project sites where services are delivered to participants. But ethnography begins with the initial approach to the entire project. In evaluation, various ethnographic skills are essential to obtain an understanding that extends beyond the actions and motivations of project operators and participants to project administrators and contracting agencies that mediate the delivery or evaluation of projects.

An ethnographic evaluator will typically first make contact with individuals in agencies sponsoring the evaluation who, although they may understand generally that "ethnography" or the "culture" concept are important, rarely grasp the broader anthropological perspective. But sponsors are often receptive to imbibing anthropological ideas if these are presented judiciously.

Because "the field" also comprises the sponsoring agency, contractor organization, and indeed, the project's philosophical focus itself (e.g., education, prevention, youth development), ethnographic skills can and should be employed prior to making site visits. Field preparation includes examining relevant literature (published accounts as well as "fugitive" sources such as grant applications, planning documents, memos, and previous evaluation reports) that can reveal the multiple cultural contexts within which projects operate.

Ethnographic skills are also needed to discover the sponsor's emic view of the evaluation, since this group of stakeholders will ultimately be the one that advocates most strenuously for the use of evaluation results on a policy level. This group also represents the evaluator's immediate "client" with which the evaluator will work throughout the project. It cannot be emphasized enough that these stakeholders are simultaneously key informants and collaborators whose perceptions, expectations, and beliefs should be studied.

The results of these preliminary inquiries can be summarized, written up, and given to primary stakeholders in a concise report or memo. Gaps, inconsistencies, or misunderstandings should be negotiated with the goal of achieving relevant evaluation.

Ethnographic Methodology

Despite some commonly held views, anthropological ethnography has traditionally employed at least some quantitative methods (e.g., census taking, household income measures, indices of crops produced as contrasted with nutritional intake, incidence and prevalence rates of disease). Certainly, a sharp opposition exists between predictive quantitative methods and processual qualitative methods seeking to depict phenomena as grounded in their naturally occurring contexts. In many evaluations, however, ethnography of the traditional anthropological kind, using multiple methods and viewing certain qualitative and quantitative methods as complementary, rather than contradictory, is essential to serving the inquiry.

There are times when evaluation stakeholders will expect to receive some findings generated in numbers that articulate well with many policy makers' views of research and, moreover, that offer quick snapshot portrayals of projects. There are also times when stakeholders wish to know about life in the project as service deliverers and participants experience it. In these cases, an anthropological ethnographer possesses the experience to know when to use which sets of methods, the flexibility to convert basic qualitative data into simple descriptive statistics, and the wisdom to interpret, differentiate, and gauge the utility of each.

Contract evaluation often requires evaluators to make relatively brief (e.g., from one to two days to as much as several weeks) visits to project sites. For the anthropologist working within a traditional fieldwork paradigm, such short-term research may appear a folly at worst or a severe constraint at best. The anthropological extended fieldwork experience has often been compared to a rite of passage that transforms the ethnographer into a bona fide anthropologist (see Agar 1980, 1986; Peacock 1986; Turner 1986 for discussion), but the ways in which this experience sharpens the anthropological ethnographer's subsequent ability to locate key informants, establish relevant questions, and identify key data sources within collapsed time periods have received little attention.

An experienced anthropologist thus may, in fact, not find such a brief field stay to be a problem. Spradley (1980:29–30), for instance, posits a spectrum of ethnographic inquiry ranging from macro to micro concerns. Macrolevel investigations attempt to comprehend a culture within all of its nested contexts of numerous communities and institutions. Microethnographies often focus on single social situations and can be profitably executed in much shorter time periods (see also Hymes 1978).

In short, the original fieldwork experience well instructs anthropologists in a wide range of methodologies (e.g., unobtrusive observation, participant observation, in-depth interviews, focus group interviews, mapmaking, genealogies, social relationship charts, content analysis, photographs, and standardized questionnaires) that can well form the basis of rapid ethnographic inquiries (van Willigen and Finan 1991).

Data Handling

The fundamental analytical mode for ethnography is to discern recurring patterns in perception, thought, statement, and behavior. Anthropological ethnographers know that data collection and analysis constitute a dialectical, iterative process. Anthropologists are experienced in recording field notes daily and in reflecting often and systematically on them so that new avenues of inquiry may be identified. Anthropologists use data like a compass: tacking back and forth between ground that has been covered in the discovery of phenomena and new directions the data point to allow the ethnographer to pilot the investigation into appropriate, but hitherto unforeseen, areas.

Anthropological ethnographers seek to elucidate many cultural patterns including social conflict, cultural contradictions, informal techniques of social control, managing interpersonal social relationships, acquiring and maintaining status, and solving problems (Spradley 1980:152–153). It is the elucidation of such patterns that makes ethnography particularly well-suited to formative evaluation, which attempts to determine the effectiveness of emergent and developing programs (see Scriven 1967). Such analysis helps in clarifying the cultural themes evident in different spheres (those of sponsors, developers, administrators, service deliverers, and participants) surrounding the operation of projects and in uncovering areas of programmatic convergence, divergence, compatibility, and incompatibility.

Ethnographic evaluators often assume that achieving "thick description" requires them to present their findings in a similarly "thick" narrative. But "thick" is not the same as "dense." Geertz's term "thick description" is often curiously separated from the essay in which it occurs: "thick" means that one should *render an interpretation,* not endlessly catalogue every descriptive detail (Geertz 1973).[5]

Experienced anthropologists know that, in addition to description, ethnography requires analysis and interpretation. Textured description entails showing as well as telling. Summaries of events are balanced with recreations of scene settings so that readers can relive the experience. Analysis involves first arranging data in an orderly, usable format and reducing them to constituent elements. Interpretation involves deciding what the data mean, explaining the results, and attaching significance to the findings. The resulting ethnographic depiction uses the description-analysis-interpretation trinity like the figure-ground reversal pictures used by psychologists. That is, each element (description, analysis, and interpretation) possesses distinctive form and content, but the shape of each depends upon the others' contours in order to produce an overall gestalt.

Evaluators are expected to go a step beyond description, analysis, and interpretation, however, in order to answer the question: what do these findings mean for policy decision making? Scriven (1993) deplores ethnographic evaluators' tendency to load reports with description without making evaluative conclusions. He terms this style "escapist and unrealistic," and likens it to "a physician who runs all of the office tests on a patient, orders all of the laboratory tests and X rays, and then gives the printouts to the patients" (1993:62).

The tough task of evaluation research is to be evaluative. Many ethnographers, particularly anthropologists, resist this because we are taught that making value judgments violates cultural relativism and runs the risk of ethnocentrism.[6] Certainly, there is the chance that well-meaning (and not-so-well-meaning) visitors ignorant of local lifeways may do harm to stakeholders (see, for example, van Willigen 1986). On the other hand, many postmodernist anthropologists (contributors to Clifford and Marcus 1986 and Fox 1991; Marcus and Fischer 1986) remind us that every act of anthropological investigation is implicitly an act of cultural critique. It cannot be otherwise, if only because anthropology is a comparative and translating enterprise.

The anthropological style of careful and informed description, analysis, and interpretation has much potential for rendering carefully articulated evaluative statements. Of special note is the anthropological ethnographer's ability to unpack actors' concepts, words, and assumptions and to devote attention to actors' situated views of reality. Indeed, as one evaluation research sponsor recently observed to me, "Someone is going to be evaluating these programs anyway—better an anthropologist because you have the ability to explain well what's happening from multiple frames of reference."

Presentation of Results

Anthropological ethnographies have traditionally consisted of bulky narratives intended for academic audiences and disciplinary peers. Most anthropologists learn to write ethnography by studying, imitating, and attempting to creatively surpass "classic" ethnographic texts. Similarly, an excellent way to learn to construct an evaluation report is to examine reports done by the sponsoring agency that are deemed "good" by those stakeholders.

An evaluation report, like any other specialized text or cultural artifact, possesses some distinguishing ritualized features, and stakeholders will expect the report to conform to certain conventions. These include a lucid style; the active voice; short paragraphs; primarily deductive logic; tables, charts, graphs, sectional breaks, and bulleted summary points; and an executive summary highlighting the main points. In order to encourage administrators and decision makers to actually read and absorb reports, ethnographic evaluators should become adept at using visually appealing (but still information-rich) tables, charts, graphs, figures, and maps. These formats can condense large amounts of information and permit readers to apprehend meaning quickly. They also break up otherwise monotonous narrative, thereby appealing to readers likely to be inundated with printed materials. Miles and Huberman (1994) is a rich source of relevant examples. Data presentations need not be limited to formal reports, however. Just as anthropologists have traditionally used several creative reporting media (such as oral presentations, slides, photographs, film, and tape recordings), so can ethnographic evaluators.

Recommendations are a common feature of evaluation reports. Frequently, both evaluations and ethnographies are inherently *deconstructive* in many of their aims and claims to elucidate "truth." Investigation requires careful inquiry of different assumptions, thoughts, perspectives, and behaviors by teasing them apart and examining them in detail. Of course, one must also synthesize an integrated picture of what occurred.

But evaluation frequently possesses an additional constructive mandate in the crafting of insightful, useful, and feasible recommendations, something in which anthropologists are rarely trained. More often, even applied anthropologists are socialized to "just let their research stand for itself," and its dissemination via published venues is considered to constitute adequate closure in terms of the investigator's responsibility in assisting practitioners.

But in contract evaluation the dichotomy between research and application is not so sharply drawn. Time constraints, multiple responsibilities, and the political structures of roles often make it difficult for stakeholders to take the lead in drafting recommendations. There are also occasions when stakeholders are genuinely looking for new ways to pursue solutions and welcome external perspectives. Besides, if anthropologists wish to influence decision making, or praxis, offering informed recommendations is a practical strategy preferable to simply presenting administrators with research results and hoping they will make the connections for themselves. Furthermore, anthropologists need not worry that offering such guidance amounts to an insidiously disempowering activity. Without a doubt, evaluators need to consider carefully the political ramifications of their recommendations.[7] The fundamental point is that when all is said and done, clients will either accept or reject an evaluator's advice; but if the evaluator does not provide any advice (or only results), the opportunity to influence praxis is severely diminished.

Again, anthropological evaluators possess a distinct advantage here because of our ability to understand and appreciate the view of each stakeholder and to advocate for marginalized groups. When making recommendations, anthropologists and stakeholders need to be aware that anthropological evaluators are bound by various codes of ethics: the American Anthropological Association's, NAPA's Anthropologists' Ethical Guidelines for Practitioners, and the American Evaluation Association's draft document on guiding ethical principles. The anthropological evaluator should ensure all stakeholder rights and should forthrightly discuss this process with sponsors and clients.

Working with Stakeholders

Anthropological fieldwork requires that anthropologists become part of the host community, even if only briefly. Fieldworkers traditionally have been advised to take it slowly initially, lest they stumble unwittingly into ill-considered political alliances or are coopted into roles laden with hidden and threatening ramifications. Fieldworkers often do encounter informant attitudes that have been shaped by the quality of their previous contact with outsiders.

When evaluators go into the field they usually find that "evaluation" carries loaded meanings for diverse stakeholder groups. This is partly due to the fact that dozens of formal evaluation models exist (for examples, see Patton 1986, 1990; Rossi and Freeman 1993). Furthermore, each stakeholder group understands different connotations of evaluation. For example, evaluation may provide data to help policy makers reach decisions; it may justify an administrator's decision to extend or terminate a project; and it can show administrators how challenging the job of project operator is or allow participants to tell how the project has (or has not) benefited their lives.

Nevertheless, for most stakeholders, "evaluation" is an anxiety-producing phenomenon. No one much likes to be judged by others, especially by outsiders. Evaluators thus typically face an array of attitudes, from acceptance to apathy to hostility, that can be stressful and require substantial patience, sensitivity, and acumen.

There are numerous beneficial roles for qualitative evaluators to assume throughout the evaluation process. These roles include collaborator, trainer, group facilitator, politician, organizational analyst, internal colleague, external expert, methodologist, information broker, communicator, change agent, diplomat, problem solver, and creative consultant (Patton 1986:319). Anthropological ethnographers are especially well positioned to become proficient in three role areas: communication, negotiation/collaboration, and facilitation/teaching.

1. *Communication:* Most anthropologists have had to learn how to do research communicating in foreign languages or subcultural dialects. Ironically, though, these same researchers may ignore these language lessons when doing contract research. It is not uncommon for researchers with advanced academic degrees to restrict themselves to "ivory tower" linguistic registers when working in public arenas. Effective anthropological evaluators should know the value of communicating in ways comfortable to local people.

This does not mean that the researcher should mimic stakeholders, since people can often quickly detect and dismiss such affectations. Nonetheless, stakeholders will expect researchers to appreciate their concepts and values, reflected in common expression.

2. *Negotiation/collaboration:* In traditional, extended fieldwork, anthropologists continually negotiate with people to solve practical problems, obtain information, and resolve ethical dilemmas. The ethnographer thus obtains not merely isolated facts (i.e., collection of data) but, equally important, also experience in establishing trusting relationships, lessons that serve evaluation well.

   Fieldwork also reminds anthropologists of the importance of collaboration (although subsequent academic socialization has traditionally inclined many anthropologists to mute its significance). Postmodernist writers have now decloaked the romantic image of the solitary anthropologist who sallies forth, gathers information under adverse conditions, and then spins adventurous tales. In fact, as deconstructionist critiques lay bare, anthropologists have usually collaborated (with key informants, indigenous assistants, spouses, and students) in their field endeavors (Caplan 1988; Clifford and Marcus 1986; Sanjek 1993). The importance of strengthening, not suppressing, collaborative techniques in applied anthropology has recently gained renewed attention (Schensul and Schensul 1992).

   The applicable analogy for anthropological evaluators is that rarely, if ever, do evaluators act alone. They are part of a complex orchestra of voices, needs, and desires, and as such, must exercise a considerable range of collaborative skills. To be sure, evaluators will sometimes be asked to spearhead the collaboration and sometimes to participate as equals. But they will always be asked to respect and include the perspectives of various stakeholders.[8]

3. *Teaching/facilitation:* These anthropological competencies would seem to arise less obviously from fieldwork experience than from university graduate training. Most anthropologists engage in teaching at some point in their careers. But didactic teaching styles, while often appropriate in the classroom, clash with those suitable in practitioner arenas. Among practitioners the goal is to facilitate understanding of the research without compromising each stakeholder's professional expertise. Effective facilitation thus requires a different set of skills than does didactic teaching. Since evaluators need to convey project information regularly to stakeholders, they should familiarize themselves with the pedagogical theory and practice of facilitation (for example, see Kohls 1985).

At the same time, anthropological evaluators can draw upon their field experiences to craft appropriate facilitation approaches. Deeply entrenched in the anthropological mind is the maxim "Assume the role of a child (or learner)," but less emphasized is the idea that research involves a sustained reciprocal relationship between learning and teaching. Anthropological researchers give information in order to get information. It is a highly unusual field situation where informants' curiosity about the researcher is not parlayed into questions asked about the researcher's own life and culture and where the anthropologist does not engage in such dialogue. As such, fieldworkers are usually teaching while they are learning. The task is to recall this experience and build on it for the purposes of facilitative, dynamic instruction where all participants—including the leader—engage simultaneously as learners and as instructors.

Conclusion

The fact that ethnography seeks to portray naturalistic contexts makes it very appealing to those who hold a stake in contract evaluation research. Many professionals trained in various disciplines are increasingly using aspects of ethnography to carry out such research. As Spradley and McCurdy (1972) demonstrated long ago, individuals with little or no knowledge of anthropology can still produce excellent ethnography, as can novelists, journalists, and other professionals. They suggested, however, that such ethnography (description) needs an *ethnological* (i.e., classification, comparison, contrast, and explanation) dimension in order to provide a profound understanding of the findings. It is this type of dimension that constitutes the "value added" that anthropologists can offer program evaluation.

But before evaluation contractors and sponsors will be systematically inclined to seek out anthropologists as powerfully viable purveyors of ethnography, anthropologists will have to be more forthcoming about how anthropological-style ethnography and explanation relate to the process of evaluation. In a reflective vein, such guidance will also be crucial to anthropologists. It will be important for us to state with clarity and integrity what we can and cannot offer in ways that are intelligible to stakeholders.

Much of this chapter has been an exercise in reflecting upon the practical implications our background and training bear for evaluation research. Simply put, this focus builds upon the strengths we already possess and, equally importantly, helps to establish a distinct niche for anthropology in public arenas. It has been my recent experience that several anthropologist colleagues, as well as those (including project clients and sponsors) from other disciplines, have exhibited a keen interest in deepening their awareness of how, specifically, anthropology can benefit contract evaluation research. If we can expand and illuminate that discourse for ourselves, we will be in a stronger position to offer it to the public and, hopefully, to contribute to the development of a still nascent practicing anthropology.

Notes

Acknowledgments. I would like to thank those who contributed their time and insights by participating in the interviews discussed in this chapter. Thanks also to David Rymph, who commented on a draft of this chapter, and to Mitchell Ratner and Michael Reed, who thoughtfully discussed with me several points made in this chapter.

1. The Chicago School of sociology has, of course, used essentially ethnographic methods since at least about 1915 when W. I. Thomas, Robert E. Park, and Ernest Burgess founded this domestic (and largely urban) United States research effort.

2. For recent considerations of the linkages between ethnography and qualitative research generally, see Lincoln and Guba 1985, Miles and Huberman 1994, and the many articles in LeCompte et al. 1992. For discussions about the linkages between ethnography and qualitative evaluation research, see Fetterman 1984, Fetterman and Pittman 1986, Patton 1987 and 1990, Pittman and Maxwell 1992, and Wolcott 1995.

3. This distinction first became clear to me at a conference (the same one cited in Payne-Jackson and Corsica's chapter introduction, this volume) I attended 2½ years ago that was sponsored by a consulting firm under contract (with a major federal agency) to evaluate substance abuse prevention demonstration projects. Ethnography was employed as part of the evaluation strategy, and a number of anthropologists were hired to conduct these inquiries. Several nonanthropologist professionals were also hired as ethnographers. During the conference—which brought together grantees, project-specific evaluators, cross-site evaluators and ethnographers, and federal project officers—it seemed that most of these stakeholders knew very little about ethnography of the anthropological kind. Indeed, several individuals employed by the organization sponsoring this ethnographic work stated that they liked anthropologists' reports because they found them "anecdotal" and "entertaining."

4. A more complete rendition of the results is contained elsewhere (Camino 1994).

5. According to one ethnographic evaluator (trained in psychology) whom I interviewed, "I read a lot of so called ethnographic evaluations and thick description is like raw data. . . . I think a lot of ethnographers and a lot of anthropologists are novelist wannabes but don't have the novelist's ability to weave the stuff into a story. Thick description can be interesting, but reading anecdote after anecdote makes you weary if you don't know what it all means." Wolcott (1995:90–91) also addresses this issue.

6. In general, researchers who wish to avoid passing judgment by providing description mean implicitly that the data contain both positive and negative elements. It is to both of these that policy makers' attentions must be guided, rather than being pointed in no particular direction. The danger in providing no guidance lies in inviting the indifference of decision makers.

7. Patton (1986:286–293, 333–339) cogently discusses the political realm of evaluations and the uses and misuses to which they can be put. He also empirically demonstrates that even university-based (and therefore presumably "apolitical") research takes place within a host of political contexts. Cohen and Cohen 1992, Paneth 1992, Price 1992, and Ritenbaugh 1992 also address the issue of research and political spheres in an issue of *Medical Anthropology Quarterly*.

8. This seemingly obvious statement does not deny that stakeholder groups may sometimes attempt to manipulate evaluators. Nevertheless, the guiding principles of collaborative efforts should be fairness and respect balanced with expertise, so that neither stakeholders nor evaluators unilaterally impose their views.

References Cited

Agar, Michael
1980 The Professional Stranger. New York: Academic Press.
1986 Speaking of Ethnography. Sage Qualitative Research Methods Series, vol. 2. Newbury Park, CA: Sage Publications.

1993 Ethnography: An Arial View. Draft paper distributed at the WAPA workshop on Rapid Assessment Procedures, Washington, DC, April 3.
Camino, Linda
1994 Does Anthropological Training Matter in Ethnographic Program Evaluation? Paper presented at the 93rd annual meeting of the American Anthropological Association, Atlanta, GA, December 3.
Caplan, Pat
1988 Engendering Knowledge: The Politics of Ethnography. Anthropology Today 4(5):8–12.
Clifford, James, and George E. Marcus, eds.
1986 Writing Culture: The Poetics and Politics of Ethnography. Berkeley: University of California Press.
Cohen, Barbara A., and Theodore E. Cohen
1992 When Social Science Confronts Medicine. Medical Anthropology Quarterly 6: 151–152.
Edgerton, Robert B., and Lewis L. Langness
1974 Methods and Styles in the Study of Culture. San Francisco: Chandler and Sharp.
Fetterman, David, ed.
1984 Ethnography in Educational Evaluation. Beverly Hills, CA: Sage Publications.
Fetterman, David, and Mary Anne Pittman, eds.
1986 Educational Evaluation: Ethnography in Theory, Practice, and Politics. Beverly Hills, CA: Sage Publications.
Fox, Richard G., ed.
1991 Recapturing Anthropology: Working in the Present. Santa Fe, NM: School of American Research Press.
Geertz, Clifford
1973 Thick Description: Toward an Interpretive Theory of Culture. *In* The Interpretation of Cultures. Pp. 3–30. New York: Basic Books.
Hymes, Dell H.
1978 What Is Ethnography? Sociolinguistics Working Paper, 45. Austin, TX: Southwest Educational Development Laboratory.
Kohls, Robert
1985 Training Know-How for Cross-Cultural Trainers. Washington, DC: Washington International Center of Meridian House International.
LeCompte, Margaret D., Wendy L. Millroy, and Judith Preissle, eds.
1992 The Handbook of Qualitative Research in Education. New York: Academic Press.
Lincoln, Yvonne S., and Egon G. Guba
1985 Naturalistic Inquiry. Beverly Hills, CA: Sage Publications.
Marcus, George E., and Dick Cushman
1987 Ethnographies as Texts. Annual Review of Anthropology 11:25–69.
Marcus, George E., and Michael M. J. Fischer
1986 Anthropology as Cultural Critique: An Experimental Moment in the Human Sciences. Chicago: University of Chicago Press.
Miles, Matthew B., and Michael A. Huberman
1994 Qualitative Data Analysis. Thousand Oaks, CA: Sage Publications.
Paneth, Nigel
1992 Power and Patronage in Medical Research. Medical Anthropology Quarterly 6: 147–148.
Patton, Michael Quinn
1986 Utilization-Focused Evaluation. Beverly Hills, CA: Sage Publications.
1987 How to Use Qualitative Methods in Evaluation. Newbury Park, CA: Sage Publications.
1990 Qualitative Evaluation and Research Methods. Newbury Park, CA: Sage Publications.
Peacock, James
1986 The Anthropological Lens: Harsh Light, Soft Focus. Cambridge: Cambridge University Press.

Pittman, Mary Anne, and Joseph A. Maxwell
1992 Qualitative Approaches to Evaluation. *In* The Handbook of Qualitative Research in Education. Margaret D. LeCompte, Wendy L. Millroy, and Judith Preissle, eds. Pp. 729–770. New York: Academic Press.
Price, Laurie J.
1992 A Medical Anthropologist's Ruminations on NIH Funding. Medical Anthropology Quarterly 6:128–146.
Ritenbaugh, Cheryl
1992 Ruminations on "A Medical Anthropologist's Ruminations on NIH Funding." Medical Anthropology Quarterly 6:149–151.
Rossi, Peter H., and Howard E. Freeman
1993 Evaluation: A Systematic Approach. Newbury Park, CA: Sage Publications.
Sanjek, Roger
1993 Anthropology's Hidden Colonialism: Assistants and Their Ethnographers. Anthropology Today 9(2):13–17.
Schensul, Jean J., and Stephen L. Schensul
1992 Collaborative Research: Methods of Inquiry for Social Change. *In* The Handbook of Qualitative Research in Education. Margaret D. LeCompte, Wendy L. Millroy, and Judith Preissle, eds. Pp. 161–200. New York: Academic Press.
Scriven, Michael
1967 The Methodology of Evaluation. *In* Perspectives of Curriculum Evaluation. Ralph W. Tyler, R. M. Gagne, and M. Scriven, eds. Pp. 39–83. Chicago: Rand McNally.
1993 Hard-Won Lessons in Program Evaluation. New Directions for Program Evaluation, 58. San Francisco: Jossey-Bass.
Spradley, James P.
1980 Participant Observation. New York: Holt, Rinehart, and Winston.
Spradley, James P., and David W. McCurdy
1972 The Cultural Experience: Ethnography in Complex Society. Chicago: Science Research Associates.
Strauss, Anselm, and Juliet Corbin
1990 Basics of Qualitative Research: Grounded Theory Procedures and Techniques. Newbury Park, CA: Sage Publications.
Turner, Victor
1986 Dewey, Dilthey, and Drama: An Essay in the Anthropology of Experience. *In* The Anthropology of Experience. Victor Turner and Edward M. Bruner, eds. Pp. 33–44. Chicago: University of Illinois Press.
Van Maanen, John, ed.
1995 The Ethnography of Ethnography. *In* Representation in Ethnography. Pp. 1–35. Thousand Oaks, CA: Sage Publications.
van Willigen, John
1986 Applied Anthropology: An Introduction. New York: Bergin and Garvey.
van Willigen, John, and Timothy Finan, eds.
1991 Soundings: Rapid and Reliable Research Methods for Practicing Anthropologists. NAPA Bulletin, 10. Washington, DC: American Anthropological Association.
Wolcott, Harry
1992 Posturing in Qualitative Inquiry. *In* The Handbook of Qualitative Research. Margaret D. LeCompte, Wendy L. Millroy, and Judith Preissle, eds. Pp. 3–52. New York: Academic Press.
1995 Making a Study "More Ethnographic." *In* Representation in Ethnography. John Van Maanen, ed. Pp. 79–111. Thousand Oaks, CA: Sage Publications.
Yin, Robert K.
1984 Case Study Research: Design and Methods. Beverly Hills, CA: Sage Publications.

"If a Dog Has Teeth, It Bites": The Impact of Multiple Stakeholder Perspectives in Contract Research

Gladys Levis-Pilz

While in graduate school I owned one of those "Spuds MacKenzie" dogs, an English bull terrier named Willie. Willie went everywhere with me and always caused a stir among the passersby. One Saturday I left him tied to a parking meter while I went into a store. When I came out, there was a small circle of children standing around Willie but keeping a wary distance. As usual they had all sorts of questions, like "What kind of dog is he?" "He looks like a pig!" et cetera. No one would come close to him. I tried to reassure the kids that they could pat him, he was friendly, and he did not bite. One of the older boys looked me in the eye and asked, "Does he have teeth?" I answered, "Of course he has teeth," to which he replied, "Then he bites."

Now, 20 years later, I find that this boy's simple but powerful observation applies to my experiences as a contract anthropologist. "If a dog has teeth, it bites." I have learned that some apparently benign research/evaluation situations are anything but, and I have learned that in my role as contract researcher I am also capable of inflicting "wounds," even though unintentional. This chapter shares some of my field experiences in order to contribute to the growing literature on the challenges of contract anthropology.

The Job

The contract specified that I would spend about ten days at each assigned site, absorbing as much as I could through my ethnographer's eyes about a local social service project and its community context. After leaving the field I would be expected to produce a lengthy, detailed report covering various etically derived issues of interest to my employer, a Washington, DC-based research and evaluation firm that had won a major federal contract to conduct a multiyear, cross-site comparison of some 64 community-based drug use prevention projects around the country.

My work was certainly not classical ethnography, and yet most of the subcontractor's consultant "site visitors" were anthropologists with extensive training and experience doing ethnographic research. The federal project officer who convinced his superiors to fund the cross-site study was a recent convert to ethnographic, "grounded" evaluation models. He believed that by sending ethnographers into the field, even for only ten days, the resulting reports would be closer to "thick description" than those done by mainstream evaluators.

While this could be called "hit-and-run anthropology" (Feldman 1981), with all sorts of limitations objectionable to traditional, academy-based anthropologists, it was still appealing to me. After all, it is rare to be asked to research and develop *any* ethnography-based report for federal bureaucracies, most of which still rely on quantitative analysis using standardized evaluation instruments.

I would eventually conduct three site visits, all to projects located in American Indian/Alaska Native communities. Project participation in the cross-site study was not mandatory, although projects were told that it was something of an honor to be invited, and their federal project officers strongly encouraged them to participate. The extra work required to host these sites visits was supposed to pay off for the participating projects by aiding future grant writing, allowing projects to "take stock" midway through their five-year funding cycle, and giving them an opportunity to be recognized as "worthy," possibly even "exemplary," human service projects.

In any case, their federal contacts assured project personnel that there was nothing threatening about these visits and that neither the site visitors nor their reports could jeopardize project funding. Project personnel, staff from both the funding agency and the subcontractor, and the ethnographic "site visitors" were brought together in Washington in order to meet each other, determine mutual compatibility, and begin a process of "bonding" before the actual site visit.

Two of my three site visits were quite well received, considering that I was a stranger, not so much to the broad Indian cultures I was visiting but surely to the specific communities and projects.[1] At each of these two other site visit locations, a project staff member was assigned to be my guide and mediator, interviews were arranged with key informants, and in both cases, special arrangements were made so that I would be able to observe reasonably "typical" meetings, interventions, and activities (e.g., school board meetings, advisory committee meetings, evaluator sessions with staff, and youth projects). One site visit was to coincide with the state high school basketball championship, so that I could participate in one of the most important annual community events.

My local guides at these other two site visits also accompanied me to places that I identified as important after I had been in the field for a few days (e.g., a local community college, the court handling juvenile cases, school bus routes, home visits with parents or guardians). During each site visit, I documented as comprehensive a view of project and community life as was possible during ten long, 12- to 14-hour days. My submitted reports represented my best efforts at rich, highly readable, "thick descriptions" of local life that tried to balance fairly the projects' components, both the more and the less successful. All of this was, of course, inevitably filtered through my ethnographer's eyes.

The Problematic Site

The third project that I visited proved to be an altogether different and more difficult situation. This project had a unique and highly creative set of core interventions set contextually in the traditional community culture, which was grounded in subsistence practices that are as crucial for survival today as they ever have been. Skilled, adult community members ("elders" as well as younger adults) worked with groups of middle-school-aged youth (ages 10–14) to teach them traditional subsistence skills. The project's objectives were to create intergenerational bonds and to reconnect youth to their community while teaching them practical skills. Funding agency representatives and other observers, who considered this to be a powerful prevention model, wanted this project to be positively highlighted, and I was considered "lucky" to be assigned to do this site visit. But I was in for a tricky undertaking.

The project's structure and community politics presented several layers of implicitly conflicting perspectives just waiting to grab the unwary ethnographer by the leg. The community group that had created the idea for the project included a strong-willed, controversial local leader who served as project director. But this group did not write the grant proposal. This was done by a regional development agency, headquartered in a distant city, which was in the business of helping rural communities to procure grants like this one. This same agency was now administering the grant in return for overhead and staffing costs.

The dichotomy between the rural, Native community where the project was implemented and the far-away, urban grantee agency caused numerous problems. Key local project personnel responsible for the delivery of direct services, as well as some community leaders, did not totally trust this "umbrella agency," although the depth of this enmity was not clear until later. Communication between these two organizations was not entirely open; thus when representatives of the urban grantee agency claimed to speak for the local community people, they were not telling the whole story. Grantee agency staff had given permission for my site visit to be conducted, perhaps assuming that community people would "buy in" for all the reasons mentioned earlier. The federal project officer, who had a fairly positive relationship with the local project director, apparently convinced the latter that my site visit was desirable. This project director agreed, although in hindsight, it was a very reluctant agreement. She perhaps never clearly understood (or accepted) what was expected of her as a site visit host.

My site visit took place in the summer. The project director met our two-person site visit team (consisting of me, the "site visitor," as well as a "site evaluator" provided by the research firm that had hired me) at the tiny local airport, transported us to an activity site, allowed us to accompany her during some of her activities (during the first two days of our site visit), introduced us to a few important community participants, and participated in one two-hour interview (when we covered about half of the scheduled questions). After four days on site, when the second member of the visiting team left, I, the ethnographer, never saw the project director again.[2]

By this time I had become acquainted with several other community members including the mayor, who was a member of the tribe served by the project. He and his Anglo wife were quite willing to talk with me about their community. In my remaining time, I also pursued other informants at church, in the lodge where I stayed, at the mayor's house, and in the town and tribal offices. I also reviewed official state and local documents, books, and curricular materials available at the local state university branch library.

Following the site visit I spent 70 to 80 hours producing the report. Given the information and informants that I had been able to access, I attempted to present a balanced view of the project and its community. On the one hand, this particular community undeniably faces some extreme difficulties, including high rates of substance abuse, few economic opportunities, and a lack of such amenities as indoor plumbing. I also described other divisive community issues such as the town-owned liquor store, three gambling establishments, and the project director's often antagonistic working style and personality.

On the other hand, the project model *did* effectively help at least some youth, and I identified other positive "unintended outcomes" such as providing socioeconomic rewards and community recognition to young adults with exceptional subsistence skills such as fishing and trapping. Some of the community's highest risk youth were being positively involved in the project. I also described these developments.

When my draft report was submitted to the local project director, she completely rejected it as being "negative" and misleading about the overall community. Her scathing comments, which condemned all outsiders who might come to do research in her community, were personally humbling for me. The federal project officer, who wanted both to "protect" his agency's relationship with this constituent and to safeguard the belief that participation in the cross-site study was a "benign" experience, requested that I revise the report. Reluctantly, I made this revision, at my own expense.

What Happened?

There is much to be learned from this experience about doing contract research. As the story unfolded, it caused pain for me, the community, and the federal agency personnel who sent me into the field. I used to teach my students about the need to be "self-reflexive"; this experience forcefully brought that truth home to me. The lessons learned from my experience, which may be applicable to most contract research situations, include the following.

The Impact of Multiple Stakeholder Perspectives

I should first state that there were several "stakeholders" with vested interests in the outcome of this work, namely: (1) the funding agency; (2) the firm contracted to conduct the overall study; and (3) the federal project officers of the individual projects. Guba and Lincoln classify all of these stakeholders as "agents," meaning, "those persons involved in producing, using, and implementing the evaluand" (1986:40). According to Guba and Lincoln's "responsive-constructivist" approach to evaluation, these agents would be required to negotiate with the "beneficiaries" of the evaluation, that is, the grantee agency and the local community.

But such a negotiation did not happen in this instance. The federal "managerial agent" determined which projects would participate in the cross-site study, the evaluation's parameters, the questions to be researched, and the reporting format. This created what Stake (1975) might call "preordinate evaluation," that is, evaluation that emphasizes a priori project goals as evaluation criteria. Guba and Lincoln would also consider the ethnographer/evaluator to be an "agent." Yet in this situation, my work was highly proscribed. Ultimately, I found myself sandwiched between the other groups (an experience also described by Reed in his chapter of this volume). In the field I encountered three or four additional, competing views from "inside" groups that were supposedly "beneficiaries" of the project being evaluated. These included the regional development agency, several community factions, and the project director.

Both the federal funding agency and the regional development agency have established ways of communicating as well as highly structured expectations of the community project (e.g., reports, a management information system [or MIS], documentation on participation rates, et cetera). These interactions occurred regularly even though these three groups were very geographically dispersed. Staff from the regional agency (none of whom lived or worked in the project community) periodically visited the local community, although they did not participate in the daily running of the project and, hence, from the viewpoint of the local project personnel, did not really understand the project.

Some direct communications occurred between the funding agency and the community project, by means of the previously alluded to personal and professional relationships established between the federal project officer and the project director. The federal project officer embodied the formal technical requirements of the funding agency, and his project-related values incorporated an active awareness of congressional budget committee constraints and expectations. The latter were translated for the project through formalized performance expectations. He held the local project director responsible for meeting these expectations through evaluation and reporting requirements. At the same time, he also admired the project director, her indigenous culture, and the project model, and these two people had a "friendly," informal relationship.

Meanwhile, the private contractor (my direct employer) had a formal business relationship with the funding agency. The contract for the cross-site evaluation was obtained through a competitive bidding process, and the contractor had to meet funding agency expectations. In other words, the "values" of all of these agents were aligned, and the contractor hired consultant anthropologists (as well as other professionals) who could deliver the terms of the contract.

In this scenario, the ethnographer/evaluator is a consultant who—very briefly—gains access to both regional and local community groups and their documentary histories, staffs, project activities, and participants. The success of this relationship depends upon the willingness of the regional and community stakeholders to accept the contractor as legitimate and to give the ethnographer, as agent of the contractor, access to the project.

In some senses, the ethnographer is peripheral to all of the other stakeholders, a fact emphasized by the grantee conference held in Washington prior to the start of fieldwork. (See also this volume's introduction and Camino's and Payne-Jackson and Corsica's chapters for other iterations of this conference.) There, in an effort to reinforce the "nonthreatening" nature of the site visits and to give the projects some sense of control over the process, project administrators were told that they could decline their assigned ethnographers in favor of someone else whom they preferred. (Payne-Jackson and Corsica examine this issue in detail.) Such decisions had to be made during the three-day conference, and choices were limited to the ethnographers on hand. Over the three years of the contract, local project prerogatives resulted in several changes of assignments among the consultant ethnographers. Some of us began to feel as if we were being interviewed for a job without knowing exactly what the job qualifications were.[3] Such experiences made some of us feel like "company men or women" (instead of professional anthropologists), who could be assigned or transferred at the will of the "boss."

Nevertheless, once work began I developed my own stake in it, which was formally defined in scope and duration by a contract. Informally, my stake (or "investment") was to do the best job possible while remaining true to the tenets of my anthropological discipline. My personal goals might include showing how useful ethnography can be to large-scale program evaluation, furthering a career in contract research, increasing a personal store of knowledge and experience about indigenous cultures, and, perhaps in some small way, contributing to the local community by highlighting successful elements of a model based upon indigenous culture.

The funding agency stakeholders were convinced that the work with projects was "benign" and maybe even "good" for the projects, that the goals should be palatable to projects (because they allowed them to contribute to an idealized, universal goal of promoting good prevention work), and that this effort would demonstrate the value of including ethnographic perspectives in the evaluation of prevention programs. The regional stakeholders, who apparently bought into this funding agency "line," acted as if their acquiescence and cooperation spoke for the local community as well. They never revealed in advance that they themselves did not have excellent relations with the local community. Finally, the local community stakeholders just wanted to get on with their work without interference from outsiders, be they regional or national.

The strength of the informal collegial relationship between the federal project officer and the local project director resulted in an agreement to participate, although no one suspected how reluctant that agreement was or how "coerced" the local stakeholder felt. It should be obvious that this was a "value-pluralistic" context (Guba and Lincoln 1986:34) in which the ingredients, for traditional anthropology/ethnography, are, in Feldman's terms, "all scrambled: time, social context . . . mission, product expected. . . . In doing contract work for any . . . federal agency, the anthropologist is inevitably affected . . . by decisions, modus operandi, and pressures present but not always seen" (1981:227, 231). Clearly, the ethnographer would be advised to begin such research with his or her eyes open.

The Ethnographer Who Should Have Known Better

I had worked for several years with several American Indian communities as their "ethnographic evaluator." I had completed one highly successful site visit under this contract in what many considered to be a really tough community. I had also bought into the group mythology that this cross-site study's "showcasing" of ethnographic applications in large-scale program evaluation could have no "down sides."

In other words (and in hindsight), I entered this particular field setting with at least two inappropriate assumptions. The most naive of these was that the possible influences and permutations of the multiple perspectives had already been dealt with and resolved to everyone's satisfaction. The other incorrect assumption was that I could do credible fieldwork entirely through the use of key informants in a highly compressed time frame. After all, it had worked in two other settings.

Writing about People Who Do Not Want to Be in Your Story

I did not anticipate that my writing/reporting style, which had apparently enlightened, satisfied, and even entertained others, would be a problem. I just assumed that it was "good ethnographic writing." As a writer, I try to use appropriate anthropological conventions to (1) support inferences with data that have been validated through triangulation and (2) write rich, vivid descriptive passages to place the reader in the setting, much as

Geertz (1974) advised. In this instance, however, the project "audience," wary as they were about the entire research undertaking and unfamiliar with the conventions of ethnographic writing, reacted negatively to much of my text.

Several examples from my formal site visit report may illustrate what I mean:

> Sheila [not her real name], the camp cook and kitchen director, completed her chores "in public" as it were, in front of everyone in camp. She narrated the things she was doing as she went about doing them, as if giving a didactic color commentary. Sometimes there were youth participants paying attention; at other times the audience included only the adults sitting around the central area of the camp. Every once in awhile she enlisted the aid of two or three youth for specific tasks (e.g., deboning fish to make "spread" or washing dishes), during which time she would give explicit instructions and talk about how it was done in the "old days." She spoke of taking the whole group of kids on a walk in the woods to identify useful plants and herbs for cooking and medicine.

The local critics of my report took particular exception to my characterization of Sheila "completing her chores 'in public,'" which they interpreted to mean that I was "putting her down." This was the farthest thing from my mind. In the context of other remarks that I had made about the open structure of the camp where most participants sat in a large circle of seats around Sheila's kitchen area, this comment of mine had seemed quite harmless to me. In actuality, I admired Sheila's abilities and intended to "highlight" them.

In another example, I wrote about John [not his real name] being "widely recognized as the 'best' and 'luckiest' fisherman around"; these were direct quotes from several informants. But some local community leaders did not like these statements at all. They believed that John was a scoundrel because he did not carry through on a job that they had asked him to do for the project—a very long, complicated story. They did not deny his high status as an able fisherman, but they did not want anything good to be said about him in my report.

While on site I found the local project office facility to be very interesting. In my eyes, it revealed the great variety of activities that go on there. Even when unoccupied by people, these offices gave me evidence of past project work. In an attempt to evoke the feelings that these office spaces engendered in me, I described this setting in the following narrative passage:

> The [project] operates from a large corner office located in the . . . complex. . . . There are no windows and the fluorescent lights on the high ceiling shed the only light. There is a jumble of materials piled on several tables and desks and a corner where the participants have a "thrift store" for reselling old clothing that is hung on a pipe suspended from the ceiling. Notices of conferences, an

> attendance roster, two copies of a complimentary letter from a parent, newspaper clippings, copies of the [project] Newsletter, and kids' essays and artwork are tacked on walls and dividers. A PC sits on a table pushed up against the middle of one wall. [The computer was on every time I entered the office, yet I never saw anyone using it.] Fran's [not her real name] desk is located in the corner diagonally opposite the doorway; it is piled high with papers and other materials. The most interesting (and telling) items in the room are a wolf pelt, a leg hold trap, and a contraption used to hold small game for skinning.

Some local reviewers considered this description to be highly insulting: they believed that I was ridiculing them for being "messy."

As a final example, I included in my report a portion of a fascinating conversation that I had with a 12-year-old girl. The first draft of my report included the following passage:

> A conversation with a 12-year-old girl at the [project] fish camp underscored how much the (riverine) setting dominates people's perceptions of the world. I described the differences between (her home) and my home in the Southwest, trying to give her a feeling for the riverless and treeless wide-open spaces. She looked at me in wonderment and asked, "Well, how do you get around?" I do not believe it ever occurred to her that you could really go anywhere without a boat!

This girl had described for me the various ways of getting around her community during the summer, primarily by boat throughout the large river system that dominates the area. The local readers interpreted this exchange and my description of it to mean that I thought that the girl was stupid. In my revised draft of the report—which *was* accepted by local reviewers—I added in parentheses, "just as it had never occurred to me before that there was a place where cars and trucks would be useless."

Conclusion

The main lesson here is that we are naive to assume that being written about is not a big deal or that the richer and thicker our descriptions are, the better. I also realized, in hindsight, that my "audience" was the contractor and, through that organization, the funding agency. The narrative forms that I employed were not at all illuminating to the local project personnel. As someone pointed out to me later, we ethnographers usually write about people who are not in power; but how many of us have ever been described in print, and how does that feel to us?

As anthropologists, we might think about our reactions to student or workplace evaluations, particularly when they are critical about us. I did include census data and other statistics provided by the community in my report, and the resulting community description was not altogether flattering. I tried to balance this with my evocative descriptions of settings, people, and activities that revealed for me the community strengths, the people, and their culture. Yet the local audience did not respond positively to this narrative.

The ultimate question for those of us in contract research is whether or not this type of situation can be avoided. The structural relationships among the stakeholders, and the fact that the only values inherent in the structure and function of the research were management-derived, suggest not. While the project staff was not actually "coerced" into participation, neither did they have total freedom to decline. The only point of "negotiation" for them was their review of the first draft of my report. If this is commonly the case, then we contract ethnographers probably often enter communities as unwelcome outsiders, and this fact will color everything that happens thereafter.

In my case, a very complex situation was made to appear simple. A greater effort should have been made to negotiate the parameters of the undertaking, to reconcile the multiple stakeholder perspectives, and to assess the true willingness of project personnel to host the site visit. Had this been done, the outcome might have been different. At the very least, contract researchers must anticipate such situations. No matter how benign our intentions or how faithful we are to the guiding principles of our anthropological discipline, there are always those healthy teeth, perhaps hidden behind a toothy grin, waiting to sink in. I am still rubbing my ankle, and there is a community out there that may never again allow an ethnographer to visit—rabid as they think we are.

Notes

1. Over the past six years, my husband and I have evaluated projects in six American Indian communities, and we seem to have established good reputations in these communities for our general knowledge of and sensitivity toward Indian culture. In addition, pre-visit preparation included an extensive review of project documents in order to familiarize myself with project components, and I read voraciously about the site visit area as well as about the local cultural group. All of this did not make me any less of a stranger to the specific community, though it did give me a foundation on which to build.

2. I believe that the project director (with the help of other community members) purposely eluded me because, on several occasions, I actively looked for her. Under more "normal" ethnographic conditions, when I might have had several months, instead of several days, in the field, this problem might have worked itself out, and I probably would have, in the end, spent a lot more time with this very key informant.

3. The qualifications often had nothing to do with our training and expertise as ethnographers. One project that I visited, located in an extremely isolated part of a large western state, a region known for its harsh weather, "tested" me before they accepted me. They told me horror stories about greenhorn Easterners coming to their reservation who then ran away before finishing their business when they discovered how tough life was there. I was not frightened because I am not a greenhorn: I also live in the West, and my family is in the cattle business. This personal background apparently gave me legitimacy in their eyes, and we got along well after that. This experience parallels Houghton's (1981) work conducting research for the United States Bureau of Land Management in Nevada, where idiosyncratic personal characteristics (like enjoying watermelon) could determine whether or not an outsider was accepted by the local population.

References Cited

Feldman, Kerry D.
1981 Anthropology under Contract: Two Examples from Alaska. *In* Anthropologists at Home in North America. Donald A. Messerschmidt, ed. Pp. 223–237. Cambridge: Cambridge University Press.
Geertz, Clifford
1974 The Interpretation of Culture. New York: Holt, Rinehart, and Winston.
Guba, Egon G., and Yvonna S. Lincoln
1986 Fourth Generation Evaluation. Newbury Park, CA: Sage Publications
Houghton, Ruth M.
1981 Talking to an Agency: Communicating the Research Findings. *In* Anthropologists at Home in North America. Donald A. Messerschmidt, ed. Pp. 238–251. Cambridge: Cambridge University Press.
Stake, Robert E.
1975 Evaluating the Arts in Education. Columbus, OH: Merrill.

Political Correctness: Issues for Native and Nonnative Evaluators

Arvilla Payne-Jackson and Joanne Corsica

Over the past 15 years, we have helped evaluate several federally-funded projects delivering various services to low-income, high-risk families in the United States. These projects' target issues have included child abuse, substance abuse prevention, the delivery of child and infant care, and the provision of comprehensive services (e.g., mental and physical health, early childhood education, education/employment/training, and child development). We have also helped conduct evaluations of several similar community-based social service projects funded by private non-profit organizations.[1]

We have typically been hired as "ethnographic evaluators" who were expected to conduct rapid assessments, using anthropological concepts and research methods, of the sociocultural contexts of the local community-based projects being evaluated. Our resulting reports were generally "qualitative" in nature and were believed by the funding agency to complement (and help explain) the "quantitative" reports prepared by other evaluators.

We have had a growing concern about the manner in which ethnographic evaluators *are assigned* to evaluate the various local service delivery projects. Anecdotal accounts have made it clear that there is often a conscious effort by both federal and private agencies to assign evaluators to projects on the basis of "politically correct" (hereafter PC) matching by ethnicity and gender.[2] Thus, for example, an infant and maternal care project located in a predominantly African American community would most likely be assigned a "matching" African American, "older maternal-like" female evaluator. This procedure often eliminates from further consideration highly experienced and capable evaluators simply because they do not match the designated criteria.

This issue surfaced at a recent national conference when several evaluators came together and shared stories. One woman objected to the fact that she had been assigned to several projects simply because she "looked Latina," although this selection process apparently did not take into account her academic background or areas of evaluation expertise. Another experienced evaluator confided that he was quite certain that he was rarely assigned to evaluate "minority" projects because he was a "white male." Yet another white evaluator noted that she had been removed as the evaluator of an African American project prior to her first site visit because that project's director believed that local client children would not talk to a white evaluator.

Several evaluators conceded that being American Indian or Hispanic does not necessarily qualify a person to evaluate all other (or, for that matter, *any other*) American Indian or Hispanic groups, since there are always multiple *intragroup* differences as well as animosities that enormously complicate the task of people studying "their own kind." These differences may jeopardize even an "indigenous" evaluator's chances of being perceived as a "fair" or "appropriate" researcher.

The evaluators' general consensus was that if this present federal trend was carried to its logical conclusion, the time might soon come when a 30-year-old, female El Salvadoran refugee would only be considered qualified to interview and evaluate *other* 30-year-old female El Salvadoran refugees of matching socioeconomic and educational background. Several evaluators' paramount concern was about the politicization and trivialization of the disciplines of anthropology and evaluation resulting from superficial decisions based upon phenotype, gender, age, and so on. Such PC practices completely overlook the fact that anthropologists are trained to be able to live and communicate effectively with people from different cultures.

Political Correctness

The PC phenomenon has grown, in part, out of the multicultural and feminist revolutions that began in the 1960s and 1970s (Ginsburg 1989; Martin 1987; Messerschmidt 1981b; Ortner 1991). A central and defining characteristic of PC behavior has been the laudable promotion of respect for diversity and for the dignity of both groups and individuals. In order to achieve this, however, PC adherents have sometimes tried to ban any expressions, ideas, or viewpoints that could be interpreted as being biased or prejudiced. This has resulted in the muzzling of individual thought and expression. The authors contend that some adherents of PC have created a situation of intellectual and practical paralysis in which everyone is afraid to say or do anything for fear of offending some unidentified entity or group or of being labeled "racist" or "fascist."

This fear of being politically *incorrect* has significantly impacted research involving poor and minority populations. Wilson (1987) discusses the research consequences of that fear in his analysis of the controversy surrounding the 1965 report written by Daniel P. Moynihan, which concluded that black urban poverty could be partly attributed to a breakdown of black family structure (Moynihan 1965). The virulent criticisms aimed at that report resulted in the curtailment for years of any serious research on inner-city minority problems undertaken by liberal scholars, none of whom wanted to be perceived as stigmatizing racial minorities. Wilson writes:

> Indeed, by 1970 it was clear to any sensitive observer that if there was to be research on the ghetto underclass that would not be subjected to ideological criticism, it would be research conducted by minority scholars on the strengths, not the weaknesses, of inner-city families and communities. . . . Thus, after 1970 for a period of several years, the deteriorating social and economic conditions of the ghetto underclass were not addressed by the liberal community as scholars backed away from research on the topic, policy makers were silent, and civil rights leaders were preoccupied with the affirmative action agenda of the black middle class. [1987:15]

In effect, PC standards increasingly function as another repressive orthodoxy, supplanting but not dismantling former modes of prejudice (Ravitch 1990). Pedersen (1994) states that one of the greatest dangers of PC ideology is "the polarization of alternatives into either/or categories. Both the advocates and the opponents of PC are in danger of oversimplifying multiculturalism by presuming a single 'correct' orthodoxy" (1994:5). He concludes that, on the one hand, the particularist may define culture too narrowly, resulting in ethnocentric exclusion by culturally defined special interest groups. On the other hand, the universalist perspective may result in continued domination by the more powerful majority culture at the expense of minority cultures.

Such issues also pertain to the populations being served by social service projects. Funding sources are often more available if the population served falls within what is perceived to be a PC category, a topic that was discussed by several staff members of one social service project who felt deeply frustrated about the required "ethnic" criteria for project participants. They questioned how effective such a practice of exclusion can be. One staff member observed that "the ultimate program would be where we could serve everyone—not pick and choose kids, but treat each and everyone alike." As another staff member put it, "The hardest thing we do is turn people away because their children don't meet our target criteria. We want to serve all children, but especially [ABC] children."

A staff member at another community project expressed this frustration as follows: "It's really hard to say no to children who ask for and need help and we have to say no. . . . It's the hardest thing I do . . . This program is needed especially by [XYZ] children who have different values."

This "either/or" exclusiveness of PC ideology may have serious repercussions for client populations, especially when the funding precludes services to some children and families *living within the same community* because they do not meet the dominant culture's PC criteria (Asad 1973; Friedman 1992; Jones 1970; Weeks 1990). A participant in one evaluation noted,

> There is nothing for kids—any kids—in these communities to do. If they don't have anything to do they get involved in alcohol and drugs. I think our intervention would be stronger and more consistent if we included both groups of kids in the program, and the kids would be able to learn from each other.

> Excluding one group of kids from the intervention is inconsistent with what we're trying to teach kids about all humans being important and valued—and then we exclude the one group of kids who want to join.

Unfortunately, the PC social-service agenda is often culturally and intellectually restrictive and blind to alternative inclusive proposals and solutions. Rather than utilizing the benefits of both insider and outsider participation and considering how both minority and nonminority groups lend insight into need-based projects, PC ideology and practice limit evaluation where differences (and the ability to incorporate those differences) could make an important contribution. This limitation (in the face of great need) is what has caused the outpouring of criticism from evaluators, the range of which has barely been touched in the foregoing discussion. Our task is to bring down these limitations by reevaluating the function and purpose of PC practice in professional evaluation.

Issues for Ethnographic Evaluators

Evaluators employed to conduct "qualitative" evaluations are now often referred to as "ethnographic evaluators," a term that will be used in this chapter. Our use of this term does not imply that we believe that such evaluators are necessarily doing, or even perceive themselves to be practicing, true ethnography.[3] Rather, they simply employ a wide variety of ethnographic techniques to produce "qualitative" reports.

In order to more clearly understand some of the problems that have been caused by such PC attempts to match evaluators and local community projects, it is important first to review certain issues central to the "insider/outsider" debate that is taking place in anthropology. While ethnographic evaluators are not doing classic ethnography, our underlying assumption is that the insider/outsider debate is, nevertheless, relevant here.

Overview of Insider/Outsider Issues

In recent years, anthropologists have debated the strengths and weaknesses of "insider" versus "outsider" ethnography.[4] Major issues concern the effectiveness of both the "insider" and the "outsider" in conducting ethnographic work and, by extension, ethnographic-based evaluations. Clearly, both approaches permit varying viewpoints and more-or-less effective project evaluations, distinguished by the vantage point from which the evaluator is reporting (Jones 1995).

Proponents of insider research claim that insiders: (1) blend into situations more easily so that interactions are more natural and wide-ranging (Aguilar 1981:19; Messerschmidt 1981b:8); (2) generally have greater linguistic competence and can better read nonverbal indications of subjective states (Aguilar 1981:18; Mascarenhas-Keys 1987:183); and (3) are less likely to make subjects feel the need to conceal their behavior and points of view (Aguilar 1981:18). According to Freilich's definition of natives, "[O]ur speech, dress, eating and sleeping habits, interactions, social relations and personal identification all approximate community norms" (1970:2).

Criticisms of insider evaluation include: insider or member knowledge leads to subjective involvement on the part of the native researcher (Aguilar 1981:15); insiders are too familiar with their surroundings, which results in a "lack of curiosity essential to research" (Aguilar 1981:16); insider research is inherently biased and promotes group interests (Aguilar 1981: 16); insiders have a more stressful impression management problem, particularly if they belong to a minority that is in a "state of enmity" with the larger society (Aguilar 1981:21; Mascarenhas-Keys 1987:181); as a professional, the insider may not be perceived as special, exotic, or powerful and, in terms of data collection, this may make people reluctant to answer questions that they perceive to be irrelevant (Aguilar 1981:21; Mascarenhas-Keys 1987:185); insiders often face higher expectations on their social and cultural performances (Aguilar 1981:21; Mascarenhas-Keys 1987:180–181, 186); insiders' own class-related aspirations (e.g., for educational achievement) may make them more acculturated to the majority rather than the minority group (Aguilar 1981:22); and insiders may be perceived as a threat in that they are trying to access knowledge that could be used for personal gain or turned against the local residents (Mascarenhas-Keys 1987:185).

Proponents of outsider research maintain that: outsiders have the advantage of being able to stand back and "abstract from the behavioral data a society's unconscious cultural grammar as well as record its conscious vocabulary" (Aguilar 1981:15; see also Foster 1972); an outsider's "strangerness" allows him or her to enjoy freedom from local commitments and to be more objective (Aguilar 1981:16; see also Beattie 1964:87); outsiders are frequently perceived as neutral confidants who have nothing personal to gain from the information they gather (Mascarenhas-Key 1987:185; see also Berreman 1972 and Goffman 1982); and the asymmetrical power relationships between an outsider and the community allow for greater access to "secret" (e.g., occult) information and opinions because outsiders are perceived to lack motives for using information against local informants (Aguilar 1981:16–17; Mascarenhas-Key 1987:185).

Criticisms of outsider evaluation include: outsiders lack access to local member knowledge, and consequently, their research can only be superficial (Aguilar 1981:15); culture shock may cause the outsider to withdraw from a situation rather than pursue it out of curiosity (Aguilar 1981:17); an outsider's nonnative status limits the range of activities in which she or he may participate (Aguilar 1981:18); and subjects will be less open with outsiders because of their perceived access to gossip networks (see Goldsmith 1989–90; Goodwin 1980; Hall 1993; Yerkovich 1977) and/or their perceived "state of enmity" (Aguilar 1981:17).

Evaluative Issues

It is important to determine if an evaluator, whether insider or outsider, is serving the interests of the local client group. As discussed earlier, having an insider evaluator does not guarantee that local community interests will be served. As Jones points out, "Since different, and sometimes conflicting, interests exist in most social groups, it is not always clear just whose interests are being served" (1995:60–61). This is particularly true when evaluators are members of indigenous elite groups that may benefit differentially from the inequities of local social stratification. Jones also points out that the choices he makes as a "native anthropologist" are not necessarily based on his "nativeness," but rather on quite separate political and ideological grounds (1995:62).

The underlying assumptions of PC agendas posit that, first, "native" evaluators are "better able" to do an evaluation because they are working with their "own people," and, second, that native insiders are better able to provide an "authentic" evaluation than are outsiders. These assumptions are rooted in an earlier period of anthropology when anthropologists were distinguished as either "nonnatives" (outsiders) or "natives" (insiders), distinctions that were perceived to be fixed, stable categories (Cerroni-Long 1995; Jones 1970; Lowie 1937; Narayan 1993). In either case, anthropologists were described as those who study and write about cultures (foreign or their own) after spending many months or even years in the field "coming to know" the studied people. Native anthropologists were assumed to be able to write about their own people from a distinctly advantageous position of intimacy (Narayan 1993:672).

The term *native* itself has also been presented as a static status, defined as "a person who is born in (and thus belongs to) the place the anthropologist is observing or writing about" (Appadurai 1988:36–37). Such precise definitions ignore the fact that no person's status is defined by a single characteristic, but rather by a composite of characteristics allowing individuals to relate variably to different circumstances. As Narayan notes, "Factors such as education, gender, sexual orientation, class, race or sheer duration of contacts may at different times outweigh the cultural identity we associate with insider or outsider status" (1993:672).

When government agencies make PC evaluator assignments based upon presumed "insider" or "native" characteristics, these choices appear to be made, in part, using the specious assumption that the "native" individual will be able to render an "unproblematic and authentic insider's perspective" (Narayan 1993:672). This assumption ignores the fact that some "natives" (because of preferential education or higher social class) may also be very "distant" from the target population. Consequently, such a "native/insider" may be perceived locally as virtually an "outsider." Given the short time frames of many evaluations, this does not leave either the insider or the outsider much time to gain the trust and confidence of local project participants. It also ignores the high quality of relations and commitment that savvy, experienced "outsiders" may have developed with communities, often resulting in their hard-won achievement of virtual bicultural status.

The assumption that an insider automatically duplicates completely the culture of the informants and, therefore, represents the authentic voice of that culture, presumes that the group being analyzed is homogenous. But the fact is that the researcher's social class, gender, and perceived identity within the ethnic group directly impact both his or her access to and rapport with the research community and the substance of the data collected. For example, while conducting research in Jamaica, one of the members of the research team wore his hair in dreadlocks (i.e., "dreads"). On several occasions, older Jamaicans were very uncomfortable talking with this person due to the negative associations they held about Jamaicans who wear dreads. As a result, these informants gave only minimal responses to his questions.

These issues of representation and authenticity also influence intracultural variation, social class, and ethnic differences *within* the community-based projects being evaluated (for detailed discussions see Aguilar 1981; Appadurai 1988; Cerroni-Long 1995; Friedman 1992; Messerschmidt 1981a; Narayan 1993). Although an evaluator may be perceived by a granting agency to be a member of a particular ethnic group representing a specific geographical area, group membership, *as defined by the local community being evaluated,* may be quite different. Factors such as family power, mixed ethnicity, and birth status may affect local perceptions of group membership. At one particular site, for example, family membership was important in defining project staff members' insider/outsider status and influence. As one staff member put it, "Family X is kind of in the 'out group' in terms of power, and person Y is not really accepted by the community, so whether the program itself will continue is questionable." The status[es] assigned to an evaluator by the people they are working with can have a direct impact on the evaluator's ability to access the needed data to effect an evaluation (Mascarenhas-Key 1987; Narayan 1993).

A second staff member pointed out that both ethnicity and family membership affect one's status, since "down here there's a bias against mixed [ethnicity]—even though they may be relatives, they aren't friendly . . . your worst enemy is your family."

At another site, one person discussed the effects both of his mixed ethnicity and of his out-of-wedlock status:

> People here are prejudiced. Not just against A but against each other. . . . I was an "out-of-wedlock" child. My mother was A, and my father was F. Some

> people accept me as F, and some don't. It affected me for a long time. . . . People here are prejudiced—not just against A, but against each other . . . a lot of prejudices and biases. That's where education and information come in.

As evidenced above, gross ethnic classifications by the dominant culture overlook the finer and frequently more exclusionary *within-group* classifications. Subsequently, the degree of ethnic mixture may affect a person's perceived legitimacy as spokesperson for a project. One interviewee, in discussing this issue, raised the same question that several other staff members were asking concerning the legitimacy of one of the teachers:

> Who are the appropriate purveyors of cultural knowledge is a delicate issue for the program, even though the staff is [classified as] 100 percent black, they are part black/part American Indian, part black/part Mexican, part black/part white, but the trainer is part black/part Chinese and the others question his legitimacy in teaching.

The staff questioned his legitimacy because he was an acculturated part black/part Chinese who identified more with his Asian heritage than with his African heritage. Ethnic identification is obviously not easy to resolve, and attempts to satisfy all parties by ethnically matching an evaluator with a particular project to be evaluated may become all but impossible.

Appeals to authenticity ignore the complex makeup of ethnic groups and the role of power and politics in defining relationships both *within* an ethnic group and *between* the group and the outside world. West, addressing this issue of racial "authenticity," argues,

> Any claim to black authenticity—beyond that of being a potential object of racist abuse and an heir to a grand tradition of black struggle—is contingent on one's political definition of black interest and one's ethical understanding of how this interest relates to individuals and communities in and outside of black America. In short, blackness is a political and ethical construct. [1993: 39]

Appeals to authenticity are played out and subverted in the politically charged arena of representation. Examples of this can be seen in the opposition that many American Indian groups encounter from other already recognized American Indian groups when they seek official recognition. The established groups claim that they are authentic and that others are not.

Policy Issues

The common federal practice of matching evaluators with projects on the basis of selected criteria is, as noted, associated with an ideology of authenticity—"Proper natives are somehow assumed to represent their selves and their history, without distortion or residue" (Appadurai 1988:37). This practice, however, ignores the fact that human social identities are transformed as people move across and through varying sets of communities, each with its own social concerns and power relations. This is brought out in Narayan's discussion of insider/outsider identity:

> Even as insiders or partial insiders, in some contexts we are drawn closer, in others we are thrust apart. . . . I would argue that every anthropologist exhibits what Rosaldo has termed a "multiplex subjectivity" with many crosscutting identifications. . . . Which facet of our subjectivity we choose or are forced to accept as a defining identity can change, depending on the context and the prevailing vectors of power. [1993:676]

Insiders and outsiders face different challenges. The insider is constantly challenging multiple norms and values, thereby assuming multiple identities. The challenge faced by outsiders is to become, at the very least, marginal natives (Mascarenhas-Keyes 1987:180).

American society is largely heterogeneous, not homogeneous, and is characterized by various types of internal variation resulting from such factors as class, geographic location, urban/rural residence, ethnic identifications within subcultures, and so on (Pelto and Pelto 1978). PC practices often overlook such complexities and operate on an unconditional either/ or basis, as described by Aguilar:

> The extreme arguments both for and against insider research rest on an implicit model that characterizes all researchers as either absolutely inside or outside a homogeneous sociocultural system. The facts indicate, however, that because no one participates in all segments (or levels) of a domestic population or shares with everyone in that population all ideational components of its culture . . . , a more realistic model of the situation would view the local ethnographer as relatively inside (or outside) with respect to a multiplicity of social and cultural characteristics of a heterogeneous population. [1981:25]

Our task of identifying the hidden assumptions of federal PC practices in selecting ethnically matched evaluators for government and private contract work can lead to sounder, more socially equitable selection processes. Such processes would avoid the fallacy of using either/or selection criteria, and appeals to authenticity would be relegated to the social and political contexts from which they actually originated. To this end, Carby argues as follows:

> The cultural, political and social complexity of black people is consistently denied in those strands of feminist and multicultural theory that emphasize "difference" and use it to mark social, cultural, and political differences as if they were unbridgeable human divisions. But this theoretical emphasis on the recognition of difference, of togetherness, requires us to ask, different from and for whom? [1992:12]

This underlying motif resides in broader issues of social and political power struggles with which both insider and outsider evaluators must grapple in order to benefit the clients of projects being evaluated.

Summary

However well-intentioned the practice of ethnic and gender matching, such faulty and oversimplified assumptions are clearly prejudicial and may represent a form of racially motivated reverse discrimination. Such an approach does not reduce prejudice or foster authentic multicultural thinking, since the practice's underlying assumptions are grounded in a narrow view of culture that precludes the search for similarities and common ground among peoples of different cultural groups.

Both insider and outsider evaluators offer their own strengths, with neither role being inherently superior. Aguilar (1981:24) focuses attention on what is perhaps the most critical determinant of evaluation success (or failure): talent. Shami (1988) adds that both the insider and outsider "depend on good data in order to theorize well and it is the process of data collection" that is important (1988:115).

Aguilar also stresses that anthropologists who have "exercised powers of empathy and perspicacity and social skills have been enabled to make use of the wider human condition." He does not deny that "cultural differences present problems for cross-cultural communication and understanding, but [states that] cultural boundaries are not hermetic seals" (1981:24).

The PC practice of evaluator matching also risks trivializing the discipline and training of anthropologists. It oversimplifies the realities of our multicultural society. PC matching of evaluators to projects results from social and political power struggles taking place within our society. As stakeholders—not only within anthropology but within society at large—we are all desirous of maintaining both research integrity and human rights in a pluralistic society.

It is therefore imperative to continue to confront the inconsistencies inherent in the discriminatory decisions that, if not reversed, may result in government agencies utilizing evaluations conducted only by "insiders," which would be no more effective than evaluations conducted only by "outsiders." Cerroni-Long proposes a timely solution by stating that comparative analysis of "native and nonnative anthropological analyses of the same settings permits us to get a better grasp of the type of culture-specific biases that affect both insiders and outsiders" (1995:10). We would be wise to follow her advice.

Notes

1. The foci of these projects ranged from an assessment of community strengths and needs in a housing project for the purpose of community-based on-site renovation and development to the evaluation of programs on community and youth development.

2. Although we hesitate to call this an official, written "policy" (and we do not use the term *policy* in this chapter), there is no doubt that some federal agencies (perhaps anticipating pressure from local grantees, who are often given the power to veto evaluator assignments) expect their contractors to "match" evaluators with projects on the basis of such factors as ethnographic skills, research orientations, cultural backgrounds, language abilities, gender,

and ethnicity. In fact, the federal contract described in this volume involved a kickoff, three-day meeting when staff from local grantees were explicitly invited to "interview" their assigned site visitors to determine the "suitability" of the latter. We should also note that de facto policies can be unwritten as well as written.

3. Hammersley and Atkinson describe what an ethnographer does: "The ethnographer participates, overtly or covertly, in people's daily lives for an extended period of time, watching what happens, listening to what is said, asking questions; in fact collecting whatever data are available to throw light on the issues with which he or she is concerned" (1983:1–2). They also point out that there is no consensus among anthropologists as to what the salient feature of ethnography is—that is to say, locating cultural knowledge (Spradley 1980), the study of patterns of social interaction (Gumperz 1981), the holistic study of societies (Lutz 1981), description in the form of storytelling (Walker 1981), or developing and testing theory (Denzin 1978; Glaser and Strauss 1967).

4. See, for example, Aguilar 1981; Appadurai 1988; Cerroni-Long 1995; Cheater 1987; Gupta and Ferguson 1992; Messerschmidt 1981b; Narayan 1993; Shami 1988; Srinivas 1966, 1976; and Srinivas et al. 1979.

References Cited

Aguilar, John
1981 Insider Research: An Ethnography of a Debate. *In* Anthropologists at Home in North America: Methods and Issues in the Study of One's Own Society. Donald Messerschmidt, ed. Pp. 15–26. Cambridge: Cambridge University Press.

Appadurai, Arjun
1988 Putting Hierarchy in Its Place. Cultural Anthropology 3:36–49.

Asad, Talal
1973 Two European Images of Non-European Rule. *In* Anthropology and the Colonial Encounter. Talal Asad, ed. Pp. 103–118. New York: Humanities Press.

Beattie, John
1964 Other Cultures: Aims, Methods and Achievements in Social Anthropology. New York: Free Press.

Berreman, Gerald D.
1972 Behind Many Masks: Ethnography and Impression Management. *In* Hindus of the Himalayas: Ethnography and Change. Gerald D. Berreman, ed. Pp. xvii–lvii. Berkeley: University of California Press.

Carby, Hazel V.
1992 The Multicultural Wars. Radical History Review 54:7–18.

Cerroni-Long, E. L.
1995 Introduction: Insider or Native Anthropology? *In* Insider Anthropology. NAPA Bulletin, 16. E. L. Cerroni-Long, ed. Pp. 1–16. Washington, DC: American Anthropological Association.

Cheater, Angela P.
1987 The Anthropologist as Citizen: The Diffracted Self? *In* Anthropology at Home. Anthony Jackson, ed. Pp. 164–179. ASA Monograph, 25. London: Tavistock.

Denzin, Norman K.
1978 The Logic of Naturalistic Inquiry. Social Forces 50:166–182.

Foster, George
1972 A Second Look at Limited Good. Anthropological Quarterly 45:57–64.

Freilich, Morris
1970 Fieldwork: An Introduction. *In* Marginal Natives: Anthropologists at Work. Morris Freilich, ed. Pp. 1–37. New York: Harper and Row.

Friedman, Jonathan
1992 The Past in the Future: History and the Politics of Identity. American Anthropologist 94:837–859.

Ginsburg, Faye
1989 Contested Lives: The Abortion Debate in an American Community. Berkeley: University of California Press.

Glaser, Barney, and Anselm Strauss
1967 The Discovery of Grounded Theory. Chicago: Aldine.

Goffman, Erving
1982 The Presentation of Self in Everyday Life. Harmondsworth, England: Penguin.
Goldsmith, Daena
1989–90 Gossip from the Native's Point of View: A Comparative Analysis. Research on Language and Social Interaction 23(2):163–194.
Goodwin, Marjorie H.
1980 "He-Said-She-Said": Formal Cultural Procedures for the Construction of a Gossip Dispute Activity. American Ethnologist 7:674–695.
Gumperz, John
1981 Conversational Inference and Classroom Learning. *In* Ethnography and Language in Educational Settings. Judith L. Green and Cynthia Wallat, eds. Pp. 3–23. Norwood, NJ: Ablex.
Gupta, Akhil, and James Ferguson
1992 Beyond "Culture": Space, Identity, and the Politics of Difference. Cultural Anthropology 7:6–23.
Hall, Joan K.
1993 *Oye Oye lo que Ustedes no Saben:* Creativity, Social Power and Politics in the Oral Practice of *Chismeando.* Journal of Linguistic Anthropology 3:75–98.
Hammersley, Martyn, and Paul Atkinson
1983 Ethnography: Principles in Practice. London: Tavistock Publications.
Jones, Delmos
1970 Toward a Native Anthropology. Human Organization 29:215–259.
1995 Anthropology and the Oppressed: A Reflection on "Native" Anthropology. *In* Insider Anthropology. NAPA Bulletin, 16. E. L. Cerroni-Long, ed. Pp. 58–70. Arlington, VA: American Anthropological Association.
Lowie, Robert
1937 A History of Ethnological Theory. New York: Holt, Rinehart, and Winston.
Lutz, Frank W.
1981 Ethnography—The Holistic Approach to Understanding Schooling. *In* Ethnography and Language in Educational Settings. Judith L. Green and Cynthia Wallat, eds. Pp. 51–64. Norwood, NJ: Ablex.
Martin, Emily
1987 The Woman in the Body: A Cultural Analysis of Reproduction. Boston: Beacon Press.
Mascarenhas-Keyes, Stella
1987 The Native Anthropologist: Constraints and Strategies in Research. *In* Anthropology at Home. Anthony Jackson, ed. Pp. 180–193. ASA Monograph, 25. London: Tavistock.
Messerschmidt, Donald, ed.
1981a On Anthropology "At Home." *In* Anthropologists at Home in North America: Methods and Issues in the Study of One's Own Society. Pp. 15–26. Cambridge: Cambridge University Press.
1981b Anthropologists at Home in North America: Methods and Issues in the Study of One's Own Society. Donald Messerschmidt, ed. Cambridge: Cambridge University Press.
Moynihan, Daniel Patrick
1965 The Negro Family: The Case for National Action. Washington, DC: United States Department of Labor.
Narayan, Kirin
1993 How Native Is a "Native" Anthropologist? American Anthropologist 95:671–682.
Ortner, Sherry
1991 Reading America: Preliminary Notes on Class and Culture. *In* Recapturing Anthropology. Richard Fox, ed. Pp. 163–189. Santa Fe, NM: School of American Research Press.
Pedersen, Paul
1994 A Handbook for Developing Multicultural Awareness. Alexandria, VA: American Counseling Association.
Pelto, Pertti, and Gretel Pelto
1978 Anthropological Research: The Structure of Inquiry. New York: Cambridge University Press.

Ravitch, Diane
1990 Multiculturalism Yes, Particularism, No. The Chronicle of Higher Education, October 24: A44.
Shami, Seteney
1988 Studying Your Own: The Complexities of a Shared Culture. *In* Arab Women in the Field: Studying Your Own Society. Soraya Altorki and Camilia Fawzi El-Solh, eds. Pp. 115–138. Syracuse, NY: Syracuse University Press.
Spradley, James P.
1980 Participant Observation. New York: Holt, Rinehart, and Winston.
Srinivas, Mysore N.
1966 Some Thoughts on the Study of One's Own Society. *In* Social Change in Modern India. Mysore N. Srinivas, ed. Pp. 147–163. Berkeley: University of California Press.
1976 The Remembered Village. Berkeley: University of California Press.
Srinivas, Mysore N., A. M. Shah, and E. A. Ramaswamy
1979 The Fieldworker and the Field: Problems and Challenges in Sociological Investigation. Delhi: Oxford University Press.
Walker, R.
1981 On the Uses of Fiction in Educational Research. *In* Practising Evaluation. David Smetherham, ed. Driffield, England: Nafferton.
Weeks, Priscilla
1990 Post-Colonial Challenges to Grand Theory. Human Organization 49:236–244.
West, Cornel
1993 Race Matters. Boston: Beacon Press.
Wilson, Julius W.
1987 The Truly Disadvantaged: The Inner City, The Underclass, and Public Policy. Chicago: University of Chicago Press.
Yerkovich, Sally
1977 Gossiping as a Way of Speaking. Journal of Communication 27:158–164.

Commentary: Three Key Issues for Elaboration

Phillip R. Herr

As an anthropologist who has been conducting evaluation research for ten years, I am pleased that NAPA is sponsoring this bulletin on federal contract research. Part of my interest in this topic stems from my work (for the U.S. Congress) in the General Accounting Office (GAO), where I conduct research similar to that done by this volume's authors, although I do not oversee contracts. The preceding chapters also address more practical concerns, which I share, about the fate of anthropology. When I completed my PhD program years ago, there was little such literature available, and I thus felt that my colleagues and I were clearing our own paths through the applied research jungle. We were part of the large group that Reed identifies that has, whether by choice or by necessity, left academia to pursue other opportunities.

I would like to focus now on these preceding chapters rather than on the wider evaluation research literature. I may perhaps be able to elaborate on several issues, embellishing them with examples from my own experience.

Incorporating Anthropology Early in the Research

McKenna and Camino, in their respective chapters, provide reasoned, dispassionate advice about the whys and hows of being an anthropologist conducting contract research. Their observations are generally consistent with my own. I would like to expand a bit on one issue, namely, the use of anthropology at the time when evaluation research is being *initiated.* I say this because all of the authors described the relatively short 5- to 12-day periods when they conducted their fieldwork. My point is not that more time in the field is the answer (although it is often useful). Rather, what is crucial is the timing of when the anthropologist is brought into the overall study. This is crucial because, as Light et al. (1990) observe, you cannot fix by analysis what you failed to do in designing the study.

It is essential to bring anthropology into the evaluation during the planning stages. It is difficult to tease out lessons after the fact when incomplete information is all that is available. This was made clear to me several years ago when a colleague described a problem that his contract research firm had encountered. This firm had constructed a methodologically tight evaluation of a social service intervention. Program clients had been randomly assigned to control and experimental groups with the assumption that some differences between them might be unambiguously attributed to the intervention.[1] After several years, however, conventional statistical analysis did not demonstrate any differences between these two groups. In an effort to salvage the study design, it was suggested at this late date that perhaps an anthropologist could examine each site's records to discern some qualitative or ethnographic pattern that might shed light on the (unrevealing) quantitative data—and on the lack of differences between the two groups.

While I did not want to discourage this person from believing that an anthropologist could be of assistance in such a study, I was compelled to remind him that the best time to have brought such a person into the evaluation would have been much earlier, when the methodology was being specified. By incorporating an ethnographic perspective into the overall research itself, much more could have been gained. The lesson for anthropologists is that having a larger and longer-term role, preferably beyond brief site visits, will be crucial when it comes time to draw the conclusions and make the recommendations.

Working with Postmodern Stakeholders

An important postmodern theme of these chapters is the considerable attention being given to involving stakeholders in the evaluation process. This is a vital aspect of good research and evaluation. What I found disconcerting was the negotiation that often occurred about the anthropologist's finished products, site visit reports in this case. Levis-Pilz's chapter about how "thick description" can go awry was particularly candid and useful in understanding this dynamic. When she described how she was asked to rewrite her report, I felt compelled to defend her right—and the right of those who follow her along this path—to record her observations in a relatively candid manner.

McKenna's chapter takes a different view of the same topic by stating that contract and postmodern ethnographers alike hope to "develop and present an effective dialogue that will simultaneously satisfy the ethnographer, the informant, and the stakeholder" (p. 38). Perhaps this view reflects what Reed summarizes in his chapter's conclusion, namely, that anthropologists are struggling with fundamental questions about the nature of our enterprise. If practicing anthropologists are to take on the hard issues, perhaps I should ask what the researcher's response should be when the postmodern ideal of satisfying everyone's needs cannot be met. More specifically, if a project is not meeting a local community's needs, is the anthropological evaluator to turn a blind eye so as not to offend? Likewise, should the ethnographer feel constrained to point out the funding agency's programmatic weaknesses that may be impeding local service delivery? While there is considerable room for negotiation in this kind of research, there is also an ethical and professional line that should not be crossed.

Keeping everyone happy is sometimes simply not possible and, in my experience, not always advisable.

Levis-Pilz's chapter also honestly appraises the give and take with stakeholders that occurs even before going into the field. She describes how project directors were given the opportunity to meet the anthropologist *before* the site visit in order that ethnographers might be accepted, rejected, or "traded in" for others. At one level, this raises some questions about features of the overall evaluation design and practice that one would be wise not to replicate. More fundamentally, Levis-Pilz also raises important concerns about how to quickly negotiate a role in the local community.

I must also point out what I think is a gap in this volume, that is, the *coordination and management* of anthropologists doing this kind of work. In his chapter, Reed describes the realities of the contract research workplace, where teamwork is the norm and collaboration is crucial if large projects are to be completed. He also alludes to the liminal state of practicing anthropologists, a state somewhere between the university where they were trained and the world in which they live and work.

At a practical level, I believe that it would be fruitful for others to discuss this very topic in a future NAPA Bulletin, particularly those in a position of managing anthropological fieldworkers on such projects. I recall a description offered by a colleague from the Washington Association of Professional Anthropologists (WAPA): this person stated that managing anthropologists is akin to "herding cats." There may be an interesting article waiting to be written on this matter, too.

I want to commend Payne-Jackson and Corsica for raising the issue of political correctness (PC) as manifested in the matching of evaluators with projects based on ethnicity and/or gender. They take on an issue that should be of keen interest to practicing and academic anthropologists. Their discussion reinforces the importance of recognizing the fluid and shifting contexts in which applied and practicing research is conducted, with its insider/outsider problems and multiple stakeholder agendas. It has been my experience that professionally trained anthropologists—regardless of their ethnicity or gender—when equipped with the requisite language ability and cultural knowledge can make significant contributions to such work. To state otherwise is to ignore much of the anthropological record.

Anthropologist, Evaluator, Qualitative Researcher

At the 1994 American Anthropological Association meetings where these chapters were first presented, I commented on the use of ethnography by nonanthropologists, a trend that I urged those in attendance to factor into their professional presentation of self. I recalled the opportunity I had several years ago to hear a prominent practitioner of federally funded evaluation research describe his work, which was heavily quantitative.

After several days of discussion, presentations, and give-and-take with participants in this class, he finally admitted that an elegant time-series model had been unable to describe why a specific government program had not had a measurable impact in the target community. He then suggested that evaluation researchers should become "closet" anthropologists when confronted with such findings: they should venture, notepad in hand, into the streets, businesses, and local government offices to obtain grounded data that their statistical models and theories had been unable to capture.

I offer this story not to make light of what struck me as a reasonable attempt to broaden the evaluator's methodological tool kit. Rather, I repeat it to remind anthropologists that we must continue to reach out across disciplinary boundaries and educate our colleagues in other fields about the positive benefits of bringing our expertise to bear on today's pressing problems.

Notes

Acknowledgments. The views expressed here are mine and do not represent the policy or the position of the GAO.

1. In many cases, a causal model is implicitly used by firms conducting contract research. This approach is often very different than that of anthropology. Anthropologists should be aware of it because it is into this framework that their results are often fit.

Reference Cited

Light, Richard J., Judith D. Singer, and John B. Willett
1990 By Design: Planning Research on Higher Education. Cambridge, MA: Harvard University Press.

Commentary: The Postmodern Link between Academia and Practice

Michael Agar

It is not so easy reconstructing something live out of texts. Scripts are not the same as the performance; scores, no substitute for the concert. Much of what happened at the 1994 AAA annual meeting session that was the source of this volume is hard to find now, including things I said in the role of discussant, inspired by the colleagues who wrote these chapters.

At the same time, I am honored that those colleagues asked me to discuss again. What I would like to do is play a riff off the issues they raise and consider what they have taught me in what may, at first glance, seem to be a peculiar light. In the map of anthropological roles that Michael Reed drew (see Figure 1 of his chapter), the academic was not much considered; understandably so, given the authors and the audience. I would like to revisit that role for a moment with the goal of backlighting the model of anthropological work in a world of power and conflicting demands, a model that includes academics as well.

Where do I stand in all of this? I claim a "pomo" (postmodern) pedigree with the best of them. I am still a tenured professor (for a few more months anyway) who does consulting. Now I am leaving that academic job and turning into what I think of as a one-man think tank, though it is usually called consulting or small business. I am listed as a half-time employee with a Washington, DC–area consulting firm, and I have also worked outside the university as a full-time federal and state employee.

So, having established my right to talk, sort of like the arrival scene in traditional ethnographies, what do I have to say? I am struck by the variety of roles that contract research involves, the complexities of their interactions, and the many trails through the decisions that they entail. This kind of "buzzing blooming confusion" perhaps inspired the authors in this volume to think in terms of "postmodern" in the first place.

But as I read across the chapters, across types, across specific issues that echo the early days of applied anthropology as well as recent postmodern debate, I start to suffer the heartbreak of the modern mind in a postmodern world. I want to dig out the common threads that run across the chapters, to include the academics in the patterns as well, to do the kind of analysis that I think of as Michel Foucault in living color, to show power and resources steering us all.

I would like to look at the academic side of the story, look with the benefit of experience and reduced vested interest because of my own decision to do another kind of role. My experience is limited to large state institutions rather than private colleges and universities, a fact that I am sure makes a difference.

A tenured professor is high on security but low on resources. Because of the security, everyone has great plans for what he or she can do, for free. One day I want to calculate the government subsidy that academics provide with all their cheap-to-free consulting services. One day I would like to cost out the time spent on all those journal and grant reviews, promotion and tenure evaluations, and personal time spent to do things that one's annual review depends on, a review that might get you another couple of bucks a month in a good year. One day I would like to calculate the money other departments and colleges save by sending their students to anthropology departments for courses, training, and consultation on ethnography and culture. "We need to run the university like a business," I hear over and over again from academic pundits. Fine by me. When do we really start?

Then there is what you are supposed to do. Most academics know how to teach and teach well. Most also know that good teaching is not cheap. But shriveling resources mean more students with fewer faculty, more undergrads in a class, more grads asking for time one does not have, more outside students discovering culture whose calls cannot be returned. Then there are committees—university, college, and department—with agendas that range from triage to unrealistic plans (given lack of resources) and nothing in between.

My favorite joke about academic life is that I am the highest paid secretary inside the Beltway, or that I am a middle-level manager without any clerical support. My favorite joke about academic anthropology is that it is a discipline whose members will fight mightily against the exploitation of everybody's labor but their own.

But still, there is all that security, compared to most everyone else in the world, and as the old saying goes, the three great things about teaching are June, July, and August. Material security and some open time: how close to heaven can you get? True enough, no argument with that, two aspects of the academic life I miss when I am not in it.

Even here, though, one should not forget the model that drives the chapters in this book. As soon as you work inside the boundaries of a discipline, a pantheon watches over your shoulder. Their living representatives sit with journals and grant givers and academic publishers and decide who to let in. I remember the thunderclap during my brief but meteoric career on a subcommittee of the National Research Council: "My God" (I was referring to Pierre Bourdieu), I realized, "this place is just a high-priced consulting firm that pays its consultants in prestige."

And those glorious summers. I am fortunate, since I was able to take advantage of the time to do something interesting and unpaid. But many colleagues—I would guess it is the statistical norm—look at summer as time to continue the economic struggle, to seek out summer teaching or project work to pay the mortgage and the kids' tuition.

I am featuring the negative here for a reason. Maybe life is different at Harvard; that I do not know. But from what many colleagues at state institutions tell me, the academic life is far from the intellectual idyll that most outside imagine it to be. More security to be sure; more encouragement to publish, no doubt. But in an age when more and more anthropologists work in roles like those described in this volume, is it still the center of things? Should it be?

My view is that academic life has become so limited and limiting, caught up in economic shifts and outdated traditions, that it now labors under the kinds of constraints that counter the old notions of "academic freedom." This leads me to think of the academic role in the same postmodern field as the different kinds of practitioner roles that the authors in this volume represent. And this, in turn, makes me wonder about our time-honored distinctions between different kinds of anthropologists.

I think that the post–World War II split in the United States between academic and applied anthropology was a historical mistake. The contributions to this book, together with my informal complaints about academia, suggest that, under the charter of "postmodern," we can glimpse a framework to see across what we have learned to think of as different segments of the field. We are all serving as crew on the same yellow submarine.

The crew all deal with some similar issues. First, anthropology features a model of traditional ethnography out of sync with current realities, an issue as true of academics as it is of practitioners. By that traditional model, no one does "real" ethnography anymore. Second, we all work in a world of interconnections across differences, a world of multiple and discordant expectations about who we are and what we produce, a world that we have to deal with, whether we like it or not, in order to be able to work at all. Third, our era of blurred identities and fluid groups affects us as much as our subjects and insures that our professional expertise will not go uncontested and that those not similarly trained will claim it. Fourth, we have learned to see the material basis of power and authority that holds meaning and context in place, for our subjects as well as ourselves. That material basis limits what it is we can do and say within the field that it defines.

Such issues—others could be listed—define the nature of anthropology's current crisis. The chapters in this book, as well as other anthropological discussions, feature them now, both inside and outside the university. What is not so frequent is to notice that these issues span all the professional roles that anthropologists occupy, in the university and outside of it.

None of this should be taken to mean that there are not important differences, although even here, the situation is a little more convoluted than we usually think. The tenured anthropology professor has a degree of job security most of the world cannot imagine. Then again, so does the career government employee. Then again, neither of them have as much as they used to now that we are in the current era of "downsizing." And it is clear, to visit for a moment that hell on earth, the land of nontenured faculty, that they face a working world loaded with others' demands, one with decision guidelines that would be an organizational embarrassment anywhere outside of an academic meeting. And finally, some colleagues are employed for academic piecework, a course here, a course there, payment that averages out to less than minimum wage, and no benefits at all.

But do not get me wrong. Underlying whatever similarities are unearthed in our unified postmodern view are critical differences. There is remarkable variation in security, with tenured academics and permanent government employees at one end of the scale, the unemployed at the other, and lots of space in between. A regular paycheck, health benefits, and a pension at the end obviously and powerfully shape perception of and response to the shared postmodern issues of anthropological work.

The point is this: Scattered across the contributions in this volume are common concerns born of outmoded ethnographic models in postmodern worlds, of control by sources of power and money, of those sensitive "others" who may articulate an "anti-you" ideology, of bewilderment at what kind of professional expertise we now represent, of buffeting by other perspectives, of the war over competing interpretations among those who have a stake in the outcome.

These are postmodern issues, all right, but they are not just limited to those anthropologists who practice rather than preach. In fact, they are not just limited to anthropologists. These issues, I think, would benefit by more collective discussion, a discussion that removes the old barriers born of U.S. anthropology's history of isolating applied and practicing work. The discussion cannot turn a blind eye to the critical issue of personal economic circumstance, but at least it can recognize this issue for the material question that it is and blend it in with the common conditions of postmodern work that all of us share.

Further, the "blurred genres" of anthropological work also suggest some rethinking of the categories of academic, applied, and practitioner. There are economically secure practitioners and insecure academics, first of all. But perhaps more interesting, should not the source of many new ideas to reshape the field come from those outside the university? Who has time to publish, some will say. Of course, some academics say the same. What about the concept of "intern," an established concept out in the world, a concept that easily lends itself to student training? And are not those outside the university engaged in teaching in some fundamental way? In my experience, at least, such "students" are, on the whole, more interested and interesting than those in the average academic classroom.

By one set of definitions—problematic in and of themselves—academics teach and do research on discipline-specific issues and are paid by a university; applied do research on societally defined issues both inside and outside the academy; and practitioners do organizational work outside the university. The dimensions here are source of income, role of research, and source of the question of concern. It strikes me, after reading these chapters and reflecting on my own checkered academic past, that these dimensions—and other issues already mentioned—define a common field of struggle as we adapt an outdated field to a postmodern world, and that they blur an old way of thinking about different kinds of anthropologists in a way that is more productive than confusing.

What we are left with is a view of a field that "decanonizes" the ivory tower, renders it more permeable, and elevates the knowledge and experience of those working at a distance from it. We are left with issues of anthropological work in a postmodern world that call for a mix of theory, research, and practice that cuts across distinctions born of anthropology's traditional academic past. And we are left with critical variation among anthropologists in their power and authority to handle such issues that—following an old insight—rest on the material basis of life, a variation that also, increasingly, shows no respect for the traditional cut between the university and the so-called real world, with slave labor academic instructors on the one hand and practitioner civil servants on the other. "Postmodern" is a good intellectual charter to rethink old distinctions, which is of course exactly what it was meant to do.

About the Contributors

Michael Agar received his PhD in anthropology at the Language-Behavior Research Lab at the University of California, Berkeley. Since then he has held a number of academic and applied research positions, most recently at the University of Maryland, College Park. He is now in transition to his own consulting business, although in the best postmodern tradition, he retains an appointment in the department. Recent publications include *Language Shock: Understanding the Culture of Conversation* and the forthcoming second edition of *The Professional Stranger*. Current projects include integrating ethnography into a national and international panel on drug and alcohol epidemiology and a 60-country study of leadership in industry.

Linda A. Camino is a Washington, DC–based consultant specializing in research and evaluation for federal, public, and private human service organizations. Much of her work focuses on community and youth development, prevention programs, and national and community service initiatives. She is also a research assistant professor of anthropology at George Washington University. Her publications include *Reconstructing Lives, Recapturing Meaning: Refugee Identity, Gender, and Culture Change* (coeditor; 1994, Gordon and Breach) and articles on African American ethnomedicine and multicultural perspectives on youth development. She is now working on a USAID-sponsored project on diabetes in Jamaica. Camino earned her PhD in anthropology from the University of Virginia. Her chapter in this volume illustrates her ongoing interest in further developing a praxis-oriented anthropology.

Joanne Corsica is an assistant professor and program director with the State University of New York/Empire State College at Fort Drum, NY, a public, liberal arts institution providing educational opportunities to adult students from diverse cultural and ethnic backgrounds. Corsica has worked extensively over the last 25 years as an applied qualitative researcher in education, health care, human services, and governmental environments. Her doctoral degree (from Union Graduate School of The Union Institute) is in social anthropology and applied linguistics, with a focus on urban and applied studies. She also completed a two-year NIAAA Postdoctoral Research Fellowship with the Alcohol Research Group/Prevention Research Center, School of Public Health, University of California at Berkeley.

Phillip Herr is a senior evaluator at the federal General Accounting Office (GAO) in Washington, DC. He has been at GAO for seven years and has managed research focusing on a broad range of international and domestic issues. Prior to joining GAO, he was an applied researcher in New York City at a management consulting firm and at the city's board of education. He earned his PhD from Columbia University's Joint Program in Applied Anthropology. His dissertation research was conducted in Central America, and he has also undertaken fieldwork in Europe and the Caribbean. His current research interests include bringing applied anthropology to a broader public policy audience.

Gladys Levis-Pilz received her PhD in anthropology from Northwestern University in 1978. Edward T. Hall was her primary mentor there; so applied anthropology has always been a focus of her work. As an assistant and later associate professor of educational foundations at the University of New Mexico, she taught courses in anthropology and education and ethnographic research methods in school settings; during her last four years there she served as department chair. This experience strengthened her appreciation of how applied anthropology can help us understand and "negotiate" institutional culture. (It also drove her out of academia!) Since 1990, she and her husband have worked as independent consultants evaluating federally funded substance abuse prevention programs. Most of these programs have been located in American Indian communities across five western states.

Margaret McKenna received her PhD in anthropology from the University of Washington in 1989. She has done contract ethnography for county, state, and federally funded programs that have included early childhood projects, family support initiatives, and studies in nursing homes. She is the principal of a small consulting firm, ConTEXT Sociocultural Research and Analysis. McKenna is on the faculty at the University of Washington and teaches health services and anthropology applied in nursing practices. She has been a consultant to agencies and has published articles on cultural variation and human services.

Arvilla Payne-Jackson is an associate professor at Howard University in Washington, DC. She received her doctorate in sociolinguistics from the University of Pennsylvania. She has conducted research and published articles in medical anthropology and sociolinguistics focusing on African American, Jamaican, and Latin American cultures. She is the coauthor of *Folk Wisdom and Mother Wit* (with John Lee) and is the producer of *African Roots to American Roots,* a documentary on African American folk medicine. She is an ethnographic consultant to various federal and nonprofit organizations and a director, producer, and scriptwriter for Experienced Media Incorporated, which produces documentaries. She is currently engaged in research on a USAID-sponsored research project on diabetes in Jamaica and is finishing two books on ethnomedicine in Jamaica.

Michael C. Reed is a practicing anthropologist who has worked since 1992 for CSR Incorporated, a Washington, DC, research and evaluation firm. He received his PhD in sociocultural anthropology in 1988 (University of Washington), following 15 months of Fulbright fellowship-funded fieldwork in francophone Africa. His dissertation was titled *An Ethnohistorical Study of the Political Economy of Ndjolé, Gabon.* Since 1990, Reed has evaluated several U.S. programs, such as youth substance abuse prevention (South Bronx, NY; Detroit; Philadelphia; West Dallas, TX; and Gallup, NM), school-age child care (Boston, Chicago, Seattle), secondary education (Bowling Green, KY; Huntington, WV), and community development corporations (Chicago). He reviews articles for the American Evaluation Association journal *Evaluation Practice.*